MEASURE FOR
MEASURE

Harvester New Critical Introductions to Shakespeare

MEASURE FOR MEASURE

Harriett Hawkins

Senior Research Fellow
Linacre College, Oxford

THE HARVESTER PRESS

First published in Great Britain in 1987 by
THE HARVESTER PRESS LIMITED
Publisher: John Spiers
16 Ship Street, Brighton, Sussex

© Harriett Hawkins, 1987

British Library Cataloguing in Publication Data
Hawkins, Harriett
    Measure for measure.—(Harvester new critical
    introductions to Shakespeare)
    1. Shakespeare, William. Measure for measure
    I. Title II. Shakespeare, William. Measure for measure
    822.3'3   PR2824

    ISBN 0-7108-1110-1
    ISBN 0-7108-0997-2 Pbk

Typeset in 11/12pt Goudy Old Style by
C R Barber (Highlands) Ltd, Fort William, Scotland

Printed in Great Britain by
Mackays of Chatham Ltd, Kent

THE HARVESTER PRESS PUBLISHING GROUP
The Harvester Group comprises The Harvester Press Limited
(chiefly publishing literature, fiction, women's studies,
philosophy, psychology, history and science and trade books),
and Wheatsheaf Books Limited (chiefly publishing economics,
international politics, women's studies, sociology, and related
social sciences).

For Josie, Marguerite, Hester and Rachel

Titles in the Series

GENERAL EDITOR: GRAHAM BRADSHAW

General Editor's Preface

The *New Critical Introductions to Shakespeare* series will include studies of all Shakespeare's plays, together with two volumes on the non-dramatic verse, and is designed to offer a challenge to all students of Shakespeare.

Each volume will be brief enough to read in an evening, but long enough to avoid those constraints which are inevitable in articles and short essays. Each contributor will develop a sustained critical reading of the play in question, which addresses those difficulties and critical disagreements which each play has generated.

Different plays present different problems, different challenges and excitements. In isolating these, each volume will present a preliminary survey of the play's stage history and critical reception. The volumes then provide a more extended discussion of these matters in the main text, and of matters relating to genre, textual problems and the use of source material, or to historical and theoretical issues. But here, rather than setting a row of dragons at the gate, we have assumed that 'background' should figure only as it emerges into a critical foreground; part of the critical endeavour is to establish, and sift, those issues which seem most pressing.

So, for example, when Shakespeare determined that *his* Othello and Desdemona should have no time to live together, or that Cordelia dies while Hermione survives, his deliberate departures from his source material have a critical significance which is often blurred, when discussed in the context of lengthily detailed surveys of 'the sources'. Alternatively, plays like *The Merchant of Venice* or *Measure for Measure* show Shakespeare welding together different 'stories' from quite different sources, so that their relation to each other becomes a matter for critical debate. And Shakespeare's dramatic practice poses different critical questions when we ask—or if we ask: few do—why particular characters in a poetic drama speak only in verse or only in prose; or when we try to engage with those recent, dauntingly specialised and controversial textual studies which set out to establish the evidence for authorial revisions or joint authorship. We all read *King Lear* and *Macbeth*, but we are not all textual critics; nor are textual critics always able to show where their arguments have critical consequences which concern us all.

Just as we are not all textual critics, we are not all linguists, cultural anthropologists, psychoanalysts or New Historicists. The diversity of contemporary approaches to Shakespeare is unprecedented, enriching, bewildering. One aim of this series is to represent what is illuminating in this diversity. As the hastiest glance through the list of contributors will confirm, the series does not attempt to 're-read' Shakespeare by placing an ideological grid over the text and reporting on whatever shows through. Nor would the series' contributors always agree with each other's arguments, or premises; but each has been invited to develop a sustained critical argument which will also provide its own critical and historical context—by taking account of those issues which have perplexed or divided audiences, readers, and critics past and present.

Graham Bradshaw

Contents

Preface

Their books are also different. Works of fiction contain a single plot with all its imaginable permutations. Those of a philosophical nature invariably include both the thesis and the antithesis, the rigorous pro and con of a doctrine. A book which does not contain its counterbook is considered incomplete.

(Jorge Luis Borges, 'Tlön, Uqbar, Orbis Tertius')

Shakespeare usually brought the subtext up to the surface and gave it to the audience directly.

(Robertson Davies, *World of Wonders*)

Measure for Measure is one of Shakespeare's most controversial plays. So far as I know, there is no single interpretation of it that cannot be countered by a dialectically opposite interpretation. Thus the more you read or think about the play, the richer, the more fascinating and the more problematical it gets. There are good reasons why this is the case. As we shall see, the script itself almost invariably includes 'both the thesis and the antithesis, the rigorous pro and con of a doctrine', even as Shakespeare himself brings various subtexts up to the surface and gives them to the audience directly. Some of the questions raised in (and by) *Measure for Measure*—for example, 'How important, or unimportant, is chastity?'—are bound to be answered, in opposite ways, by individual members of the audience, even as they are dramatically answered, in opposite ways, by individual members of the cast. In certain cases, irreconcilable disagreements have necessarily resulted from the differing personal and sexual, or theological or historical, premisses and priorities of different readers and audiences and directors and critics. For instance, depending on how you define ideal 'womanhood', you can (on the one hand) argue that the fiery, icy Isabella of the first Acts learns what it is to be a woman from the pliant, passive, patient, forgiving, submissive, supine Mariana (see pp. 106–10 below); or, on the other hand, you can argue that Isabella's puppet-like behaviour in the hands of the Duke after he takes over her destiny in Act 3 ('What is your will?', 'Show me how, good father', 'I do desire the like', 'She'll take the enterprise upon her, father,/If you advise it', 'I am directed by you', etc.) is just as infuriating as it is inconsistent.

This book is divided into three chapters dealing with the moral and dramatic problems that have generated the most heated critical controversy: these are the relationships between sex and 'sin', between temporal justice and Christian mercy, and between Shakespeare's differing modes of dramatic construction and characterisation. What the continuing controversies about all these issues would seem to demonstrate is that, because *Measure for Measure* contains its *own* contradictions, it furnishes evidence for dialectically opposite conclusions about virtually every major issue involved in the course of the action itself.

> *Claudio.*   Death is a fearful thing.
> *Isabella.*   And shamed life a hateful.

Which of the conflicting characters and arguments we, personally, concur with here must largely depend, not on what we conclude that Shakespeare—or his original audience—might have believed, but on whether we ourselves believe there to be, or not to be, such a thing as a fate worse than death. Likewise, various other questions raised about sex and sin, law and order, life and art, and the ways of gods and mortals, are extra-historical, extra-literary, and extra-dramatic and thus tend to open up (rather than to shut-off) further speculation, and to evoke (rather than put down) passionate responses to the various characters and conflicts portrayed. To modern readers, the play may seem especially significant precisely because certain questions raised in it are still wide open to dispute in everyday life, as well as in art. After all, you cannot devise a drama—or a criticism—to make people think for themselves, and then insist on doing all their thinking for them. That is why, rather than offering yet another interpretation of *Measure for Measure*, I have stressed alternative ways of thinking about its conflicts, its characters and its structure.

It seems to me that critical arguments insisting that 'we' should *not* respond to the characters, or action, in ways at odds with whatever interpretation of the play is being posited, are, in a profound sense, anti-dramatic as well as counter-productive. Indeed, such arguments would seem to constitute the best possible evidence that the play does elicit—or historically has elicited—the very responses that the critic is insisting it prohibits. There are, for instance, scholarly arguments that the marriage and pardon of Angelo should not cause any problems for critically and historically enlightened modern audiences, since they would not have caused any problems for Shakespeare's Christian audience (see p. 29 below). Yet these arguments are posited, as it were, in dialectical opposition to the cries of outrage that the ending of *Measure for Measure* has, in fact, provoked from neoclassical, Romantic, post-Victorian and modern audiences, and critics, and readers common and uncommon, Christian and agnostic, alike. Discussing the pardon and marriage of Angelo, devoutly Christian critics, who otherwise differ as much as Coleridge and Dr Johnson, use the same word 'indignation'. For Coleridge, the ending 'baffles the strong indignant claim of Justice', while Dr Johnson concluded that 'every reader feels some indignation when he finds [Angelo] spared'.

A major conflict involved in modern counter-interpretations of *Measure for Measure* is the conflict between a critical concern with those aspects of the play that tend to arouse passionate responses (such as indignation) and critical defences of the ending which attempt to defuse those responses in terms of the Duke's official resolution of the dramatic conflict between justice and mercy. Some arguments also stress the ways in which the play conforms to certain twentieth-century criteria of dramatic or poetic merit: it is thus defended in terms of its thematic unity, or hermeneutical allegory, of Brechtian alienation, or an Eliot-like detachment, or of its satirical or clinical perspective on the various vices and follies dramatically dissected on the stage. D. L. Stevenson, for instance, has argued that, throughout *Measure for Measure*, Shakespeare encourages the audience to examine the moral decisions and conflicts of the characters with 'a sardonic detachment equal to that of the Duke'. The characters, therefore, are 'deliberately simplified and made less interesting in themselves than is Hamlet, for instance, or Falstaff' (Stevenson 1966, pp. 12, 14). This last point seems true of Shakespeare's portrayal of, say, Mariana, in the second half of the play, but in the first Acts there is no dramatic distancing or insulation involved in the original portrayals of characters like Angelo, Isabella and Claudio, who have actually tended to provoke just about every kind of response *except* impersonal and clinical detachment. In cases like these, as Stevenson himself acknowledges later on, 'what is held brightly in focus is an excited and intensified sense of the immediate knowableness of a created and complex being: a Hamlet, an Isabella' (p. 120). Thus, the fact is that *if* Shakespeare really did not intend us to respond to these passionate partisans in a passionate and/or partisan way, but set out to distance our responses to them in order to achieve a kind of Brechtian alienation, then something either (a) went very wrong with the play, in so far as it has the opposite effect, or (b) there is something wrong with a critical approach to *Measure for Measure* which insists that our perceptions of the individual characters and conflicts can only be distorted by our emotions. Arguably anyway, Brechtian alienation itself is alien to a drama wherein the playwright, in effect if not intent, engages the audience emotionally, as it were by every means at his disposal, and so transforms us from witnesses to active participants in the conflicts portrayed on the stage. And it could be that the resolution of *Measure for Measure* is so contrived as to seem problematical by design on the part of Shakespeare, if not the Duke. In any case, some of the most passionate responses elicited by the characters and conflicts throughout *Measure for Measure* do seem opposed to, rather than reconciled with, or contained within, the comic ordering of events at the end. This is why, in order to defend the 'unity' of the play as a whole, certain critics have found it necessary, retrospectively, to discredit responses at odds with the ducal resolutions of the various conflicts.

Perhaps paradoxically, one very powerful modern device for getting us to suppress or deny our actual responses to the various characters and conflicts in *Measure for Measure*, including the Duke and the ending, is to imply that these responses are discreditable because they *are* 'modern', and to argue that a 'contemporary audience' in the early seventeenth century would have reacted quite differently. Of course, we cannot be certain that our own responses are anything like those of a Jacobean playgoer. But we do know that audiences, at any drama, tend to differ remarkably, from spectator to spectator, from reviewer to reviewer, from first night to matinée, from one performance to another. Shakespeare's audiences probably differed in comparable ways: certainly there is no reason to suppose that they did not. Perhaps because of, rather than in spite of, the fact that our knowledge of them is so nebulous,

Elizabethan and Jacobean audiences have proved wonderfully plastic in the hands of modern critics. The 'original audience's' responses can thus become whatever the needs of the present argument require them to become, and so they will inevitably respond to *Measure for Measure* in whatever way the present critic believes they ought to have responded to it.

The imposition of differing modern critical responses upon an imaginary 'Jacobean audience' can be illustrated by surveying various twentieth-century appeals to the authority of the audience that was present at the opening night of *Measure for Measure*. And surely there is something inherently suspect about these pleas for the support of a spectral audience that is so notably unlike any other collection of individuals ever assembled, in any theatre, before or since, to watch a play. Reading over the criticism of *Measure for Measure*, one may find the original audience transformed into a collection of churlish louts, caring nothing about the legal, social and moral dilemmas so powerfully presented before them in the opening scenes, but continually panting, thirsting and lusting for some kind (any kind) of happy ending:

> The audience were interested in the Duke's reforms only in so far as these served the plot. They did not care a straw about the triumph of his theories as a reformer or the moral welfare of Vienna. What they did wish was that the play should end, as a comedy should, in a general atmosphere of happiness.
>
> (Lawrence 1931, pp.104–5)

Query: how does he know? And if Shakespeare's audience would be perfectly satisfied by the dramatic refinements of, say, *Gammer Gurton's Needle*, why did Shakespeare confront them (and us) with a hornet's nest of legal, social and moral problems in the first place? This argument, in fact, serves to get us far, far away from the real responses that *Measure for Measure* has, as a matter of critical record, actually provoked in all sorts of people. And if the ending of *Measure for Measure* has disturbed or disappointed commentators of all types and schools—including Dr Johnson and Coleridge; A. C. Bradley and L. C. Knights; E. M. W. Tillyard and Mary Lascelles—in the eighteenth, nineteenth and twentieth centuries alike, the odds are pretty good that it might have disturbed some Jacobean spectators as well.

Even if not, even if the ghost of King James himself came back to announce publicly that the original audience viewed *Measure for Measure*, 'from beginning to end', as 'pure comedy, based on absurdity like *The Mikado*, full of topical allusions to a current bestseller [King James's own *Basilicon Doron*], and every situation exaggerated into patent theatricality' (see Bennett 1966, p.158), the recorded evidence of the more complicated response of the critical audience since then would still outweigh this statement. After all, the original audience is dead as earth, but the audience provided by the critical record survives. And perhaps it is the fittest to survive, since it includes some of the very greatest poets and dramatists over three centuries, along with a most distinguished group of critics and scholars. Thus, while the critic who argues that the original audience must have interpreted *Measure for Measure* as a hilarious farce may have a logically coherent position, the extant record of troubled responses evoked by the play ever since the opening night cannot be historically explained away. These recorded responses vary, too. And surely there are numerous ways of playing *Measure for Measure* more or less seriously, more or less lightly, with different tonalities and effects. But there should be a limit to how much any critic can use unverifiable conclusions about how the 'original audience' might have responded to deny our right to respond, freely and naturally, to the script itself.

Still reading over the criticism of *Measure for Measure*, one suddenly comes across a very different kind of

Renaissance man to whom this play is supposed to appeal. He is a solemn, pious cleric, learned 'in the grammatical tradition stemming from Sts Augustine and Bonaventura', finding the immediate sense of nature 'less important than the theological, moral and mystical lesson that it contains', reasoning by 'analogies, conformities, correspondences and mystical comparisons'. To justify his interpretation of *Measure for Measure* as an allegory of the Atonement, Roy W. Battenhouse summons forth the Renaissance counterpart of those twentieth-century critics to whom this interpretation would be most congenial (Battenhouse 1946, p.1043). In doing so, he reflects a thoroughly modern affection for the abstract, the theological, the symbolic; an affection that frequently lauds the Duke of Vienna as the embodiment as well as the agent, of Providence Divine, and extols him as a More-Than-Prospero who is beyond all mortal and moral categories of judgement. In a peculiar critical inversion common to allegorical interpretations of *Measure for Measure*, Battenhouse gives critical hosannas to the play's least successfully realised character, the misty Mariana, while its most vividly realised characters (the Angelo, Claudio and Isabella of the first Acts) get severe castigation. As will be argued later on, the Duke may well be realised in a masterly fashion, but in ways that dramatically raise, rather than answer, certain possibly *unanswerable* questions about the ways of gods to mortals, and the nature of the powers that be.

We may freely choose to concur with, or to reject, any number of conflicting views of the play, or of its original audience, depending on how much weight we give to the dramatic or historical evidence against the interpretation being posited. Obviously, any source of insight into the play is to be welcomed. But there is no external authority (theological, critical, historical or psychoanalytical) to which we may turn for a final solution to the sexual, social, legal and moral conflicts portrayed within the tragi-comedy itself. As the following quotations from the Bible and

Machiavelli will illustrate, diametrically opposite interpretations of *Measure for Measure* can, in turn, be based on its obvious affinities with the Gospels, or on its (equally obvious) affinities with *The Prince*. Likewise, differing interpretations of it may be based on its affinities with subsequent 'problem plays' or medieval morality plays or Greek drama. What I shall argue here is that the greatness of *Measure for Measure* lies not in the facility with which it may be used to confirm, but in the multifarious ways that it calls into question, the convictions most passionately maintained by its audience, its readers, its critics or its directors *off-stage*, as well as by the characters on stage. For that matter, it is difficult to think of any premiss about sex and sin, or law and order, or about art and life, or about the ways of gods and mortals, that is not dramatically challenged in, or by, a tragi-comedy that would seem, on the one hand, to suggest that human nature can—and, simultaneously, would seem to suggest that human nature cannot—be made to perform according to a scenario of the Duke's or of Shakespeare's (or of anyone else's) contriving. I shall also argue that its ability to elicit passionate responses to its characters and conflicts may be the primary source of the play's dramatic energy and power and impact on its audience.

Towards the end of this book a short survey of the ways that certain explicit or implicit permutations of the conflict between Isabella, Claudio and Angelo have been developed in successive plays, novels, operas, operettas and soap-operas from Davenant's *The Law Against Lovers* to *Dallas*, is attached as an Appendix on 'The Legacy' of *Measure for Measure*. Quite apart from being very amusing and, I believe, very illuminating, the differing permutations of the 'monstrous ransom' plot would seem to demonstrate—if any demonstration is needed—that Shakespeare knew a sure-fire dramatic situation when he saw one.

H.H.
Linacre College, Oxford

Acknowledgements

Shakespeare references are to *The Complete Works of Shakespeare* edited by Peter Alexander (London 1951). Critical interpretations from which the major arguments surveyed here were derived are listed in the Select Bibliography. Mark Eccles's invaluable *New Variorum Edition of Measure for Measure* (New York 1980) includes more comprehensive bibliographical citations of past and present arguments concerning the individual characters, the construction, the realism, the symbolism, the meaning and the message of the play.

I am grateful to the Open University for permission to use arguments and illustrations from my radio lecture, '*Measure for Measure*: Some Open Questions' (first broadcast for the course in Shakespeare in June 1984). I have previously discussed other aspects of the play, in differing critical contexts, in *Likenesses of Truth in Elizabethan and Restoration Drama* (Oxford 1972) and in *The Devil's Party: Critical Counter-Interpretations of Shakespearian Drama* (Oxford 1985). Other arguments posited here were first published in an essay on 'Virtues and Vices in *Measure for Measure*' (*Shakespeare Survey* 31, pp. 105–13—reprinted in *Aspects of Shakespeare's 'Problem Plays'*, edited by Kenneth Muir and Stanley Wells, Cambridge 1982)—and in a short article, 'What Kind of Pre-Contract Had Angelo? A Note on Some

Non-Problems in Elizabethan Drama', in *College English* 35, pp.173–9.

For offprints, stimulating arguments, answers to queries and invaluable criticism of my own criticism, I am most indebted to J.B. Bamborough, Graham Bradshaw, Eric Buckley, Dennis Burden, Cicely Havely, Christopher Hill, Derick Marsh, Juliana Michie, A.D. Nuttall and Evert Sprinchorn. And I owe special thanks to Robert Hardy, CBE, for an actor's perspective on the role of the Duke.

The Stage History

1604. The Account-Book of the Office of the Revels recorded a performance by Shakespeare's company, The King's Men, at Whitehall on December 26: 'By his Ma^{tis} [Majesty's] plaiers: On St. Stiuens night in the Hall A play Caled Mesur for Mesur: Shaxberd.' This is the only reference to a performance of the play in Shakespeare's lifetime.

1662. The Duke's Company acted *The Law Against Lovers*, an adaptation of *Measure for Measure* by Sir William Davenant, at Lincoln's Inn Fields Theatre.

1700. Another adaptation, by Charles Gildon, *Measure for Measure, or Beauty the Best Advocate*, was acted at Lincoln's Inn Fields.

1720. The first known performance of Shakespeare's original version since its opening night at Whitehall in 1604, took place at Lincoln's Inn Fields on December 8, starring Quin as the Duke, Boheme as Angelo, and Mrs Seymour as Isabella.

1701–50. *Measure for Measure* was acted 69 times in London, but other plays by Shakespeare were far more

popular—*Measure for Measure* was the seventeenth most
frequently performed of all his plays and the sixth most
frequently performed of the comedies.

Notable seventeenth, eighteenth and nineteenth-century
stars who appeared in *Measure for Measure* include
Betterton, Milward, Palmer, Daniel Terry and Hopkins
Robertson as Angelo; Quin, Kemble and Macready as the
Duke; and Mrs Bracegirdle, Mrs Cibber, Mrs Siddons and
Helena Modjeska as Isabella.

Perhaps the most famous twentieth-century production
of the play is still Peter Brook's production for the Royal
Shakespeare Company at Stratford-upon-Avon in 1950,
starring Harry Andrews as the Duke, John Gielgud as
Angelo, and Barbara Jefford as Isabella. Another notable
production at Stratford, starring Emlyn Williams as
Angelo, was directed by Anthony Quayle in 1956.

Among the movie stars who have appeared on stage in
Measure for Measure is Katherine Hepburn, who played
Isabella to Robert Helpmann's Angelo in the Old Vic tour
of Australia in 1955. The New York Shakespeare Festival
production in 1976 directed by Joseph Papp starred Sam
Waterston as the Duke, John Cazale as Angelo, and Meryl
Streep as Isabella.

Measure for Measure has proved especially congenial to
modern directors, lending itself, in turn, to permissive,
carnivalesque interpretations; to authoritarian, allegorical,
The-Duke-as-God-Figure interpretations; to Freudian and
Marxist interpretations, and so on. The emergence of AIDS
may inevitably alter subsequent theatrical and critical
interpretations of the play's references to venereal disease
and its associations between sex and death. Various recent
productions are subsequently discussed with reference to
their differing portrayals of specific characters and/or cruxes
in the action of the play.

The Critical Reception

Measure for Measure has proved more popular with twentieth-century commentators than with any previous generation of critics. The play attracted hardly any critical attention in the seventeenth century: John Dryden described the plot as 'grounded on impossibilities'. Although successive eighteenth-century commentators admired the way the unities of time and place were observed, and noted the 'fine moral reflections and discourses' within the play, there was disagreement about the relative merits of the comic and serious parts of the script. On the one hand, it was argued—then as now—that Shakespeare's efforts 'to torture the action into a comedy' resulted in 'low contrivance, absurd intrigue and improbable incidents'. On the other hand, there were—and still are—counter-arguments, such as Dr Johnson's, asserting that the 'light or comic part' of this play is 'very natural and pleasing'.

Where eighteenth-century critics were primarily concerned with the play's structure, the focus of nineteenth-century criticism shifted to the characterisation. Isabella is described as an angel of light by some critics, while others deplore her inflexibility, even as the morality of every other major character in the play becomes a subject for critical dispute. Romantic and Victorian critics found certain aspects of the play repellant: Coleridge thought that the comic and serious parts alike equally bordered on the 'hateful'; the one disgusting, the other horrible. Yet it was generally agreed that, whatever its faults, the play was, through and through, profoundly Shakespearian.

George Bernard Shaw observed that Shakespeare, in *Measure for Measure*, (as in *All's Well That Ends Well* and *Troilus and Cressida*), seemed 'willing to start at the twentieth century'. These plays could be seen as dramatic explorations of intellectual problems comparable to the 'Problem Plays' of Ibsen or of Shaw himself. And, however much they may have disagreed in other ways, twentieth-century critics have found *Measure for Measure* remarkably amenable to modern critical approaches and profoundly relevant to modern readers and audiences. Throughout the twentieth century, the number of critical books and essays devoted to the play has tended to grow, exponentially, from decade to decade, from year to year. Most of the best of all twentieth-century critics of Shakespeare have written brilliantly about *Measure for Measure*. But, as some of the arguments subsequently cited will demonstrate, so much— including this book—is currently being published about this particular play that the odds are very good that the worst criticism of any play by Shakespeare published nowadays, is likely to be on *Measure for Measure*.

These facts account for the comparatively long bibliography included at the end. To give a clear idea of the range and variety of arguments about this particular play, it has been necessary to quote extensively from a body of commentary ranging, very like the play itself, from the sublime to the ridiculous, from the best to the worst—and back again. Readers can thus decide for themselves which of the various arguments posited are the most profound, or the most ridiculous, or the most profoundly ridiculous, even as they enter their own arguments and interpretations into the lists. From neo-classical to post-structuralist criticism, this play has proved simultaneously impressive and puzzling to its admirers and detractors alike. Which parts are 'great' may be a matter of unending dispute, but the play seems to most critics to be a 'great' play in parts: nobody calls *Measure for Measure* 'mediocre' or even 'good'. And however much people nowadays might disagree with a critic of the old school such as Arthur Quiller-Couch, the majority of present as well as past members of the critical jury ruling on *Measure for Measure* would tend to agree, although they might not say so in the same words, with Quiller-Couch's observation that 'in despite that its parts do not fit ... no play of Shakespeare's carries a stronger conviction that, although the goods may be "mixed", we are trafficking with genius.'

Some Preliminary Quotations

How Dukes Use Their Deputies in Machiavelli and
in *Measure for Measure*

When the duke [Cesare Borgia] took over the Romagna,
he found it had been controlled by impotent masters ...
so that the whole province was full of robbers, feuds and
lawlessness of every description. To establish peace and
reduce the land to obedience, he decided good
government was needed; and he named Messer Remirro
de Orco, a cruel and vigorous man, to whom he gave
absolute powers. In short order this man pacified and
unified the whole district, winning thereby great renown.
But then the duke decided such excessive authority was
no longer necessary, and feared it might become odious;
so he set up a civil court in the middle of the province,
with an excellent judge and a representative from each
city. And because he knew that the recent harshness had
generated some hatred, in order to clear the minds of the
people and gain them over to his cause completely, he
determined to make plain that whatever cruelty had
occurred had come, not from him, but from the brutal
character of the minister. Taking a proper occasion,

1

therefore, he had him placed on the public square of Cesena one morning, in two pieces, with a piece of wood beside him and a bloody knife. The ferocity of this scene left the people at once stunned and satisfied.

(Niccolò Machiavelli, *The Prince*)

Duke   I have deliver'd to Lord Angelo,
A man of stricture and firm abstinence,
My absolute power and place here in Vienna.
. . . .
                             ... Now, pious sir,
You will demand of me why I do this.

Friar   Gladly, my lord.

Duke   We have strict statutes and most biting laws,
The needful bits and curbs to headstrong
        steeds,
Which for these fourteen years we have let
        slip;
Even like an o'ergrown lion in a cave,
That goes not out to prey. Now, as fond
        fathers,
Having bound up the threat'ning twigs of
        birch,
Only to stick it in their children's sight
For terror, not to use, in time the rod
Becomes more mock'd than fear'd; so our
        decrees,
Dead to infliction, to themselves are dead;
And liberty plucks justice by the nose;
The baby beats the nurse, and quite athwart
Goes all decorum.

Friar   It rested in your Grace
To unloose this tied-up justice when you
        pleas'd;
And it in you more dreadful would have
        seem'd

| | Than in Lord Angelo. |
| Duke | I do fear, too dreadful. |

Sith 'twas my fault to give the people scope,
'Twould be my tyranny to strike and gall them
For what I bid them do; for we bid this be done,
When evil deeds have their permissive pass
And not the punishment. Therefore, indeed,
      my father,
I have on Angelo impos'd the office;
Who may, in th'ambush of my name, strike
      home,
And yet my nature never in the fight
To do in slander.

                    (*Measure for Measure*, I.iii. 11–43)

Measure for Measure and the Gospels

Biblical quotations are from the King James Version
because it is easily accessible to students. The 'Measure for
Measure' passages in the translations available to
Shakespeare are not significantly different.

I

*Judge not, that ye be not judged. For with what judgment ye
judge, ye shall be judged; and with what measure ye mete, it
shall be measured to you again.*

*And why beholdest thou the mote that is in thy brother's eye,
but considerest not the beam that is in thine own eye?*

*Thou hypocrite, first cast out the beam out of thine own eye;
and then thou shalt see clearly to cast out the mote out of thy
brother's eye.*

                    (St Matthew, 7:1–5)

Escalus   Let but your honour know,
             Whom I believe to be most strait in virtue,
             That, in the working of your own affections,
             Had time coher'd with place, or place with
                      wishing,
             Or that the resolute acting of our blood
             Could have attain'd th' effect of your own
                      purpose,
             Whether you had not sometime in your life
             Err'd in this point which now you censure him,
             And pull'd the law upon you.

                      (*Measure for Measure*, II.i. 8–16)

II

And he said unto them, Is a candle brought to be put under a bushel, or under a bed? and not to be set on a candlestick?

For there is nothing hid, which shall not be manifested; neither was any thing kept secret, but that it should come abroad.

If any man have ears to hear, let him hear.

And he said unto them, Take heed what ye hear: with what measure ye mete, it shall be measured to you.

                      (St Mark, 4:21–4)

Duke   Heaven doth with us as we with torches do,
             Not light them for themselves; for if our
                      virtues
             Did not go forth for us, 'twere all alike
             As if we had them not.

                      (*Measure for Measure*, I.i. 33–6)

III

Be ye therefore merciful, as your Father also is merciful.

Judge not, and ye shall not be judged: condemn not, and ye shall not be condemned: forgive, and ye shall be forgiven.

Give, and it shall be given unto you; good measure, pressed down, and shaken together, and running over, shall men give into your bosom. For with the same measure that ye mete withal it shall be measured to you again.

And he spake a parable unto them. Can the blind lead the blind? shall they not both fall into the ditch? ... And why beholdest thou the mote that is in thy brother's eye, but perceivest not the beam that is in thine own eye?

Either how canst thou say to thy brother, Brother, let me pull out the mote that is in thine eye, when thou thyself beholdest not the beam that is in thine own eye? Thou hypocrite, cast out first the beam out of thine own eye, and then thou shalt see clearly to pull out the mote that is in thy brother's eye.

(St Luke, 6:36–42)

Isabella   How would you be
If He, which is at the top of judgment, should
But judge you as you are? O think on that;
And mercy then will breathe within your lips,
Like man new made.
. . . .
         Go to your bosom,
Knock there, and ask your heart what it doth
         know
That's like my brother's fault. If it confess
A natural guiltiness such as is his,
Let it not sound a thought upon your tongue
Against my brother's life.

(*Measure for Measure*, II.ii. 75–9, 136–41)

Measure for Measure and Christ's Teachings on Sex, Sin, Guilt and Forgiveness: Some Contradictions and Some Parallels

I On Criminality of Intent

> *You have heard that it was said by them of old time, Thou shalt not commit adultery:*
> *But I say unto you, That whosoever looketh on a woman to lust after her hath committed adultery with her already in his heart....*
> . . . .
> *For out of the heart proceed evil thoughts, murders, adulteries, fornication, thefts, false witness, blasphemies:*
> *These are the things which defile a man.*

(St Matthew 5:27–8 and 15:19–20)

> Isabella   My brother had but justice,
> In that he did the thing for which he died;
> For Angelo,
>   His act did not o'ertake his bad intent,
>   And must be buried but as an intent
>   That perish'd by the way. Thoughts are no
>   subjects;
>   Intents but merely thoughts.

(*Measure for Measure*, V.i. 446–52)

II On Women Taken in the Acts of Adultery or Fornication, and the 'Double Standard'

> *And the scribes and Pharisees brought unto him a woman taken in adultery; and when they had set her in the midst,*
> *They say unto him, Master, this woman was taken in*

adultery, in the very act.

Now Moses in the law commanded us, that such should be stoned: but what sayest thou?

This they said, tempting him, that they might have to accuse him. But Jesus stooped down, and with his finger wrote on the ground, as though he heard them not.

So when they continued asking him, he lifted up himself, and said unto them, He that is without sin among you, let him first cast a stone at her.

And again he stooped down, and wrote on the ground.

And they which heard it, being convicted by their own conscience, went out one by one, beginning at the eldest, even unto the last: and Jesus was left alone, and the woman standing in the midst.

When Jesus had lifted up himself, and saw none but the woman, he said unto her, Woman, where are those thine accusers? hath no man condemned thee?

She said, No man, Lord. And Jesus said unto her, Neither do I condemn thee: go, and sin no more.

(St John, 8:3–11)

Duke   I'll teach you how you shall arraign your
                    conscience,
              And try your penitence, if it be sound
              Or hollowly put on....
              Love you the man that wrong'd you?
Julietta Yes, as I love the woman that wrong'd him.
Duke   So then, it seems, your most offenceful act
              Was mutually committed.
Julietta   Mutually.
Duke   Then was your sin of heavier kind than his.

(*Measure for Measure*, II.iii. 21–8)

III On Forgiveness and Mercy

> *Ye have heard that it hath been said, An eye for an eye, and
> a tooth for a tooth ...*
>
> . . . .
>
> *Ye have heard that it hath been said, Thou shalt love thy
> neighbour, and hate thine enemy.*
>
> . . . .
>
> *But I say unto you, Love your enemies, bless them that curse
> you, do good to them that hate you, and pray for them which
> despitefully use you and persecute you.*

(St Matthew 5:38–44)

Duke   Against all sense you do importune her.
               Should she kneel down in mercy of this fact,
               Her brother's ghost his paved bed would break,
               And take her hence in horror.
               . . . .

Isabella [*kneeling*] Most bounteous sir,
               Look, if it please you, on this man condemn'd,
               As if my brother liv'd. I partly think
               A due sincerity govern'd his deeds
               Till he did look on me; since it is so,
               Let him not die.

(*Measure for Measure*, V.i. 431–46)

(*Measure for Measure*, V.i. 431–46)

'Measure for Measure' in *Measure for Measure*

Angelo   When I, that censure [Claudio], do so offend,
               Let mine own judgment pattern out my death,
               And nothing come in partial.

(II.i. 29–31)

Duke He who the sword of heaven will bear
    Should be as holy as severe;
    Pattern in himself to know,
    Grace to stand, and virtue go;
    More nor less to others paying
    Than by self-offences weighing.
    Shame to him whose cruel striking
    Kills for faults of his own liking!
    Twice treble shame on Angelo,
    To weed my vice and let his grow!
    . . . .
    Craft against vice I must apply.
    With Angelo to-night shall lie
    His old betrothed but despised;
    So disguise shall, by th' disguised,
    Pay with falsehood false exacting,
    And perform an old contracting.
(III.ii. 243–63)

Duke   as he adjudg'd your brother—
    Being criminal in double violation
    Of sacred chastity and of promise-breach,
    Thereon dependent, for your brother's life—
    The very mercy of the law cries out
    Most audible, even from his proper tongue,
    'An Angelo for Claudio, death for death!'
    Haste still pays haste, and leisure answers
      leisure;
    Like doth quit like, and Measure still for
      Measure.
    Then, Angelo, thy fault's thus manifested,
    Which, though thou wouldst deny, denies thee
      vantage.
    We do condemn thee to the very block
    Where Claudio stoop'd to death, and
      with like haste.
           (V.i. 401–13)

Angelo   O my dread lord,
              I should be guiltier than my guiltiness,
              To think I can be undiscernible,
              When I perceive your Grace, like pow'r divine,
              Hath look'd upon my passes. Then, good
                        Prince,
              No longer session hold upon my shame,
              But let my trial be mine own confession;
              Immediate sentence then, and sequent death,
              Is all the grace I beg.

              . . . .
              I am sorry that such sorrow I procure;
              And so deep sticks it in my penitent heart
              That I crave death more willingly than mercy;
              'Tis my deserving, and I do entreat it.
                        (V.i. 364–72, 472–5)

· 1 ·

Sex and Sin in 'Measure for Measure'
Some Open Questions

You are confusing two concepts: *the solution of a problem*
and *the correct posing of a question*. Only the second is
obligatory for an artist. Not a single problem is solved in
Anna Karenina and *Eugène Onegin*, but you find these
works quite satisfactory ... because all the questions in
them are correctly posed.... The court is obliged to pose
the questions correctly, but it's up to the jurors to answer
them, each juror according to his own taste.

(Anton Chekhov)

Where God hath a temple, the devil will have a chapel.
(Robert Burton, *The Anatomy of Melancholy*)

Where's that palace whereinto foul things
Sometimes intrude not? Who has that breast so pure
But some uncleanly apprehensions
Keep leets and law-days, and in sessions sit
With meditations lawful?

(Shakespeare, *Othello*)

Let the devil
Be sometime honour'd for his burning throne!
(Shakespeare, *Measure for Measure*)

11

In *Measure for Measure*, the internal, dramatic dialectic whereby differing questions and arguments give rise to altogether different counter-questions and counter-arguments, may explain why there is not now, and perhaps never will be, a critical concensus concerning the correct answers to any of the major questions posed in, and by, the play itself. Here, for instance, are some of the sexual, social, moral, and political questions that remain wide open to debate.

How important—or unimportant—is chastity? And what constitutes rape? How grievous a violation is it to be blackmailed or tricked into bed with someone you, personally, would not choose to have sexual intercourse with? Given a conflict between Christian virtues (like chastity and charity), which should take precedence? Should a brother allow his sister to prostitute herself in order to save him? Should a young novice sacrifice her chastity, and so jeopardise what she believes to be her immortal soul, in order to save her brother's life? And if she will not do so, should she encourage another woman to do it for her?

And what about the rule of law? Does the scriptural commandment, 'Judge not that ye be not judged' apply to princes and magistrates who are professionally bound to enforce the laws of the land? If so, *or* if not—"twas my fault to give the people scope'—is it right for the Duke to deputise Angelo to 'strike and gall' the people for what he, himself, had bid them do?—'For we bid this be done,/When evil deeds have their permissive pass/And not the punishment' (I.ii. 37–9). And what if certain laws 'set down in heaven', or on earth, conflict with the biological and psychological laws of human nature? How socially disruptive, or socially acceptable, is premarital sex? Or organised prostitution? And what about shot-gun weddings? Isn't the free consent of both parties just as important in marriage as in sex? How binding is a legal certificate if there is not a marriage of true minds?

Throughout the play, differing characters give us

conflicting and contradictory answers to such questions, even as Isabella, Angelo and Claudio dramatically give each other measure for measure concerning the major conundrum debated in their confrontation scenes. Would it be a 'sin' or an act of 'virtue', for Isabella to save Claudio by yielding to Angelo? Isabella, of course, believes that it would be a mortal sin:

> Better it were a brother died at once
> Than that a sister, by redeeming him,
> Should die for ever.
>
> (II.iv. 106–8)

Conversely, Angelo argues that there would be a 'charity' in sinning to save a brother's life, and at the Last Judgement our 'compell'd sins/Stand more for number than for accompt' (II.iv. 57–8, 63–4). Claudio himself goes even further and tells Isabella that

> What sin you do to save a brother's life,
> Nature dispenses with the deed so far
> That it becomes a virtue.
>
> (III.i. 135–7)

Isabella, in turn, insists that if her brother had any virtue, then 'had he twenty heads',

>   he'd yield them up
> Before his sister should her body stoop
> To such abhorr'd pollution.
>
> (II.iv. 181–3)

'Wilt thou be made a man out of my vice?' she asks Claudio:

> Is't not a kind of incest to take life
> From thine own sister's shame?
>
> (III.i. 139–41)

Which, if any, of these characters, or arguments, is right? Given their differing personal and moral priorities and premisses, as well as their differing vested interests and desires, are all of them, in one way or another, right? Or, given the clash between differing values and virtues (such as chastity and charity), aren't there certain cases where no single option or argument can possibly be deemed right or acceptable to all of the individuals concerned? When confronted with dramatic conflicts of this kind, we in Shakespeare's audience occupy a position comparable to that of the characters themselves, in so far as our personal situations, as well as our historically or theologically (or sexually or ideologically) based opinions about the issue may, in turn, determine which of their opinions we concur with, or reject.

So complex are the issues, so powerful are the contradictory arguments, that it would seem quite impossible to prove which, if any, of the arguments he gave to Isabella, Claudio, Angelo or the Duke was deemed to be right by Shakespeare himself. Did he, for instance, view life as a fate worse than death?

> The best of rest is sleep,
> And that thou oft provok'st; yet grossly fear'st
> Thy death, which is no more. Thou art not thyself;
> For thou exists on many a thousand grains
> That issue out of dust. Happy thou art not;
> For what thou hast not, still thou striv'st to get,
> And what thou hast, forget'st. Thou art not certain;
> For thy complexion shifts to strange effects,
> After the moon. If thou art rich, thou'rt poor;
> For, like an ass whose back with ingots bows,
> Thou bear'st thy heavy riches but a journey,
> And Death unloads thee. Friend hast thou none;
> For thine own bowels which do call thee sire,
> The mere effusion of thy proper loins,
> Do curse the gout, serpigo and the rheum,

For ending thee no sooner. Thou hast nor youth nor
    age,
But, as it were, an after-dinner's sleep,
Dreaming on both; for all thy blessed youth
Becomes as aged, and doth beg the alms
Of palsied eld; and when thou art old and rich,
Thou hast neither heat, affection, limb, nor beauty,
To make thy riches pleasant. What's yet in this
That bears the name of life? Yet in this life
Lie hid moe thousand deaths; yet death we fear,
That makes these odds all even.

                                   (III.i. 17–41)

It is hard to imagine any bleaker reasons to 'Be absolute for
death' than the ones that the Duke gives to Claudio. But
then, *mutatis mutandis*, it is difficult to imagine any better
reasons to be absolute for life than the ones that Claudio
gives to Isabella:

Ay, but to die, and go we know not where;
To lie in cold obstruction, and to rot;
This sensible warm motion to become
A kneaded clod; and the delighted spirit
To bathe in fiery floods or to reside
In thrilling region of thick-ribbed ice;
To be imprison'd in the viewless winds,
And blown with restless violence round about
The pendent world; or to be worse than worst
Of those that lawless and incertain thought
Imagine howling—'tis too horrible.
The weariest and most loathed worldly life
That age, ache, penury, and imprisonment,
Can lay on nature is a paradise
To what we fear of death.

                                  (III.i. 119–33)

Thus, on the basis of counter-quotations from the same script, individual members of the audience—very like the individual characters portrayed on the stage—may arrive at diametrically opposite conclusions about the same issue; or remain torn between conflicting attitudes towards the same thing (life, death, chastity–integrity, authority, permissiveness, the rule of law, etc.). What it is almost impossible to do is to defend any one position or character or response—or interpretation of the play as a whole—*without* arguing against another one. The critical result is a tangle of intertwined, yet mutually contradictory, interpretations of the play based on different arguments for or against the various characters, all of which can be supported by quotations from the text itself, and so would appear to be equally valid. Yet when they are looked at in isolation from each other, they also seem equally reductive, since Shakespeare himself tends to confront his (or our) strongest case in favour of someone or something with the most powerful arguments that can be levelled against it— and vice versa—as if the pros (and indeed the play) would be incomplete without their cons. The fact that Shakespeare here would seem to have felt that the major, if not the only obligation of the artist was to assure that the various questions in the play were, and are, 'correctly posed', is what makes *Measure for Measure* so fascinating; but it also makes it difficult to reach any agreement about the rights and wrongs involved, since what one character (or critic) insists is right, another character (or critic) insists is all wrong. What makes certain conflicts even more difficult for any one—or all—of us to resolve, is the fact that the major characters in the play so often contradict *themselves*.

For instance, in Act 2 Scene 3, the Duke sanctimoniously arraigns Julietta's conscience for her 'sin' in having voluntarily had sexual intercourse with Claudio, whom she dearly loves, and to whom she had been pre-contracted (I.ii. 138–42), but had not yet finally married in church:

Duke	Love you the man that wrong'd you?
Juliet	Yes, as I love the woman that wrong'd him.
Duke	So then, it seems, *your most offenceful act*
	W as *mutually* committed.
Juliet	*Mutually.*
Duke	*Then was your sin of heavier kind than his.*
Juliet	I do confess it, and repent it, father.
Duke	'Tis meet so, daughter, but lest you do repent
	As that *the sin* hath brought you to this *shame*,
	Which sorrow is always toward ourselves, not
	heaven,
	Showing we would not spare heaven as we love
	it,
	But as we stand in fear—
Juliet	I do repent me as it is an *evil*,
	And take the *shame* with joy.
Duke	There rest.

(II.iii. 24–36, my italics)

Julietta's sexual complicity (her act of love) is thus morally
held against her. Yet the identical act that is here deemed by
the Duke to be a 'wrong', a 'sin', a 'most offenceful act' to be
repented as an 'evil', is, in the case of Mariana, proclaimed
to be 'no sin' at all. 'Fear you not at all', the Duke (still
disguised as a friar) tells Mariana,

[Angelo] *is your husband on a pre-contract.*
To bring you thus together *'tis no sin,*
Sith that the *justice of your title to him*
Doth flourish the deceit.

(IV.i. 70–3, my italics)

Given the seemingly arbitrary and *ad hoc* judgements
involved in the Duke's moral about-face, it is hard to see
what, if any, common principle of morality or justice or
equity, governs his arraignment of Julietta's conscience and
the instructions and absolution he gives to Mariana. Sexual

'sin', the Duke seems to imply, is (or is not) whatever he says
it is (or isn't). It also seems as hypocritical as it seems
inconsistent—

> lawful mercy
> Is nothing kin to foul redemption.
>
> (II.iv. 112–13)

> [Better a brother died at once]
> Before his sister should her body stoop
> To such abhorr'd pollution.
> . . . .
> More than our brother is our chastity.
>
> (II.iv. 182–5)

> Mercy to thee would prove itself a bawd.
>
> (III.i. 151)

—when Isabella joins the Duke in encouraging Mariana to
play the bed-trick on Angelo: 'The image of it gives me
content already' (III.i. 250).

Yet another inconsistency involving criteria of sexual
morality, justice and judgement occurs in Act 5, when
Isabella argues that Angelo should not be subject to the
death penalty, on the grounds that, unlike Claudio, he was
guilty only 'in intent':

> *Isabella*   My brother had but justice,
> In that he did the thing for which he died;
> For Angelo,
> His act did not o'ertake his bad intent,
> And must be buried but as an intent
> That perish'd by the way. Thoughts are no
>   subjects;
> Intents but merely thoughts.
>
> (V.i. 446–52)

Isabella is certainly correct so far as Angelo's determination to force her into sexual intercourse, and for that matter, his subsequent intention to have Claudio killed, is concerned. Yet judged by the standards of her *own* judgement of Claudio, who was 'Condemn'd upon the act of fornication/To lose his head' (V.i. 70–1), Angelo remains legally subject to the death penalty, since (as a result of the bed-trick) Angelo also 'did the thing' for which Claudio appeared to have died, having, likewise, had sexual intercourse with a woman to whom he was pre-contracted, but had not finally married in church.

Indeed, when seen in terms of the obvious dramatic ironies here involved, the wheels of *Measure for Measure* appear to have turned full circle, as it were in order to ensure that Angelo would, finally, offend against the law of Vienna in *exactly* the same way that Claudio did:

> *Angelo*   'Tis one thing to be tempted, Escalus,
> Another thing to fall...
> . . . .
> You may not so extenuate his offence
> For I have had such faults; but rather tell me,
> When I, that censure him, do so offend,
> Let mine own judgment pattern out my death,
> And nothing come in partial.
>
> (II.i. 17–31)

> *Duke*   This is [Claudio's] pardon, purchased by such sin
> For which the pardoner himself is in
>
> (IV.ii. 103–4)

> *Duke*   Claudio, whom here you have warrant to execute, is no greater forfeit to the law than Angelo who hath sentenc'd him.
>
> (IV.ii. 149–50)

> Duke   as he adjudg'd your brother—
> ·
> The very mercy of the law cries out
> Most audible, even from his proper tongue,
> 'An Angelo for Claudio, death for death!'
> ·
> Like doth quit like, and Measure still for
>   Measure.   (V.i. 401–9)

Although they may be necessary to display Isabella's decision to show mercy to her enemy and (perhaps?) to persuade Shakespeare's audience that Angelo should be spared the death-penalty since his acts 'did not o'ertake his bad intent', Isabella's arguments still seem casuistical, since the legal case against Angelo remains as valid as the one against Claudio (who 'is no greater forfeit to the law' than Angelo, who sentenced him), while the moral case against Angelo is stronger far. This kind of legal and moral nit-picking would seem critically absurd with reference to another kind of play; but because the characters themselves constantly indulge in it, *Measure for Measure* positively encourages it.

For instance, in recent years there has been a concerted scholarly effort to justify the Duke's, and Isabella's, comparatively lenient judgements of Mariana and Angelo, and comparatively severe condemnations of Julietta and Claudio, in terms of legalistic distinctions between two different kinds of Elizabethan betrothal contract (*de praesenti* and *de futuro*). Yet there is no scholarly certainty concerning what kind of pre-contract which couple had. The reason for this confusion is that Shakespeare himself, as it were deliberately, describes the two pre-contracts in virtually identical ways. Here is Claudio's account of his sexual and legal relationship with Julietta:

> Thus stands it with me: upon a true contract
> I got possession of Julietta's bed.

You know the lady; she is fast my wife,
Save that we do the denunciation lack
Of outward order; this we came not to,
Only for propagation of a dow'r.

(I.ii. 138–43)

And here is the Duke's account of the contractual
relationship between Angelo and Mariana:

She should this Angelo have married: [he] was affianced
to her by oath, and the nuptial appointed; between which
time of the contract and the limit of the solemnity her
brother Frederick was wreck'd at sea, having in that
perished vessel the dowry of his sister.

(III.i. 206–9)

To demonstrate the obvious similarities consequent on the
bed-trick, one need only put Claudio's statement into the
mouth of Mariana, since the identical words describe her
situation just as accurately as they described Claudio's:
'Thus stands it with me: upon a true contract I got
possession of Lord Angelo's bed. You know the man. He is
fast my husband, save that we do the denunciation lack of
outward order. This we came not to, only for propagation of
a dow'r.'

If there is any difference between the kind of contract that
Claudio had with Julietta, and the pre-contract between
Mariana and Angelo, it is so super-subtle that one can
readily understand why 'the courts themselves in
Shakespeare's day were frequently at a loss to distinguish
between the two types of betrothal contract' (see Harding
1950, p. 149). None the less, there are numerous arguments
insisting that Shakespeare's original audience would have
realised that what was 'wrong' in the case of Julietta and
Claudio, was 'no sin' in the case of Mariana and Angelo,
since the 'type of betrothal which Claudio and Juliet had

entered upon did not in law give them any marital rights, whereas Mariana's contract with Angelo did, at least in law' (see Nagarajan 1964, p.xxx). One critic goes so far as to assert that Claudio must have been lying to Shakespeare's audience, as well as to Lucio, when he claimed to have a 'true contract' with Julietta (see French 1972, pp.17–19). But no such legal or moral distinctions are made clear in the script itself. Why not?

Assuming that Shakespeare and his original audience had, in fact, based their moral judgements on technical distinctions between betrothal contracts *here portrayed* as so much alike that any differences between them seem so insignificant as to appear non-existent, then Shakespeare— along with his original audience—could be charged with a legalism comparable to Angelo's, to say nothing of a lack of any common sense or Christian charity or normal humane compassion with regard to Claudio and Julietta ('O, let him marry her!'). For that matter, Shakespeare himself had a daughter born to him only six months after his own wedding (for further biographical associations, see Scouten 1975, pp.70–1). Moreover, two of the play's major dramatic and moral ironies get lost amidst scholarly arguments about the pre-contracts, and—arguably anyway—these ironies explain why Shakespeare dramatically stresses the similarities, not the differences, between them in the text.

1. Much of the action of *Measure for Measure* seems contrived to force Angelo to offend against the law of Vienna in the same way, and then face judgment under the same statute by which he had sentenced poor Claudio to death ('When I, that censure him, do so offend,/Let mine own judgment pattern out my death'). Having so offended, Angelo keeps his word when, in the end, he asks for the death penalty ('"Tis my deserving, and I do entreat it'). 'Like doth quit like'—with a vengeance—until Angelo is granted the mercy he denied to Claudio (for further discussion, see Hawkes 1964, p.96 and Hunter 1965, p.219).

2. Claudio's sexual relationship with Julietta does, indeed, differ strikingly from the other sexual and matrimonial relationships involved in *Measure for Measure*. But it does not differ in its legality. It differs in its mutuality. For the fact is that the act of sex between Claudio and Julietta—which, paradoxically, is the one that is most emphatically, consistently and severely condemned as sinful—is the *only* sexual act in *Measure for Measure* that was undertaken with mutual consent, prompted by mutual desire and dignified by mutual love (I.ii. 147; II.iii. 26–7). By contrast, every other act of sexual intercourse that is contemplated or consummated in it involves coercion, prostitution, pandering, blackmail, force or trickery.

The inconsistent judgements by the Duke and Isabella may have resulted from a major moral and structural conundrum; that is, how *not* to condone premarital sex in general and, simultaneously, justify (a) the bed-trick and (b) the pardon of Angelo. The 'conscience' scene between the Duke and Julietta may structurally serve to confirm Claudio's insistence on mutuality (I.ii. 147) so as to make it absolutely clear to the audience that he was not guilty of 'the forcible seduction of a virgin' (as were his counterparts in Cinthio's *Epitia* and *Hecatommithi*—see Lever 1965, pp. xxxviii, 156–8); and to show us that Julietta is not a 'loose' woman; and to stress the way that even the most venial act of illicit sex involves guilt and shame on the part of Julietta and Claudio alike:

> Claudio   As surfeit is the father of much fast,
> So every scope by the immoderate use
> Turns to restraint. Our natures do pursue
> Like rats that ravin down their proper bane,
> A thirsty evil; and when we drink we die.
>   (I.ii. 120–4)

Yet the fact remains that, even if we could find some

legalistic distinction between their pre-contracts that would allow us to do so, there is no equitable or charitable or truly just way to applaud what Mariana did with Angelo and, *simultaneously*, condemn Claudio for a sin of heavier kind than Angelo's.

What, then, *is* the relationship between sex and sin and vice and virtue in *Measure for Measure*? Which of its characters should be condemned as malefactors, or seen as more sinned against than sinning or more to be pitied than censured? It is as if, in his treatment of sex and sin, Shakespeare here set out to develop the photo-negative reversals between virtue and vice that he had previously described in *Romeo and Juliet* (II.iii. 17–22):

> For nought so vile that on the earth doth live
> But to the earth some special good doth give;
> Nor aught so good but, strain'd from that fair use
> Revolts from true birth, stumbling on abuse;
> Virtue itself turns vice, being misapplied,
> And vice sometime's by action dignified.

Throughout *Measure for Measure*, Shakespeare dramatically confronts us with specific occasions wherein 'virtue itself turns vice', while 'vice sometime's by action dignified'; even as a state of complete bewilderment concerning virtue and villainy is comically encapsulated in poor Elbow's speech confusing 'benefactors' with 'malefactors';

> *Elbow*   I do lean upon justice, sir, and do bring in here before your good honour two notorious benefactors.
> *Angelo*   Benefactors! Well—what benefactors are they? Are they not malefactors?

Elbow   If it please your honour, I know not well what
           they are; but precise villains they are, that I am
           sure of, and void of all profanation in the world
           that good Christians ought to have.
                                              (II.i. 47–55)

Can its Christian context help us to resolve the play's
conflicts, or does *Measure for Measure* itself reflect a
profound historical and enduring *uncertainty* concerning the
degree of 'profanation in the world that good Christians
ought to have'—or ought to tolerate in others? For that
matter, Christ's own teachings about sex and sin (see p. 6–7
above) seem contradictory. As Milton observed,

Where the Pharisees were strict, there Christ seems
remiss; where they were too remiss, he saw it needful to
seem most severe: in one place he censures an unchaste
look to be adultery already committed; another time he
passes over actual adultery with less reproof than for an
unchaste look; not so heavily condemning secret
weakness, as open malice.
                        (Milton [1643–8], 1959, p. 283)

In Shakespeare's own time, differing Christian de-
nominations held—just as they still hold—conflicting views
about a number of sexual and moral issues involved in
Measure for Measure. For instance, if, as St Paul insisted, 'it is
better to marry than to burn', then, Catholics argued, it is
obviously better still to renounce the flesh altogether, to
take Holy Orders or enter a convent or a monastery.
Conversely, Protestants extolled marriage, as opposed to
monasticism. And of course there were, as there always are,
some downright irreligious people around in seventeenth-
century England, and Shakespeare's audience may well have
contained (at least) a few irreverent libertines like Lucio, or
like one Thomas Webbe, who is cited by Christopher Hill

as having concluded that 'There's no heaven but women, nor no hell save marriage' (Hill 1974, p.9).

Given the course of action in *Measure for Measure*, it does seem indisputably true that to attempt to expunge all profanation from the world is to invite disaster—which is precisely what the Duke of Vienna does when he summons Angelo, a 'man of stricture and firm abstinence' to bring back the birch of law (I.iii. 11–43). As Shakespeare reminds us elsewhere (see Sonnet 94), 'Lilies that fester smell far worse than weeds'. It is, however, when Angelo crosses it that Shakespeare most dramatically erases the fine line between virtuous and vicious forms of human psychology and sexuality that may elevate men and women or degrade them. For Angelo, a man who never feels the 'wanton stings' of sensuality, but 'doth rebate and blunt his natural edge/With profits of the mind, study and fast' (I.iv. 60–1), soon goes beyond all measure in punishing sexual offenders, and his self-righteousness almost immediately begins to manifest itself in sadism: '[I hope] you'll find good cause to whip them all' (II.i. 131). 'Punish them to *your height of pleasure*', says the Duke, much later on (V.i. 238, my italics), when Angelo asks to have his 'way' with Isabella and Mariana (thus suggesting that the bed-trick failed to effect a miraculous reformation so far as Angelo's pleasure in punishing people is involved). Anyway, from the beginning of the play, the punishment of vice itself turns vicious, misapplied. Furthermore, *virtue* itself enkindles vice when the purity of a young novice ignites Angelo's desire to defile it. 'Love in thousand monstrous forms doth oft appear', wrote Spenser, and this is one of them:

Shall we desire to raze the sanctuary
And pitch our evils there? O fie, fie, fie!
What doest thou, or what art thou, Angelo?
Dost thou desire her foully for those things
That make her good?...
. . . .

O cunning enemy, that, to catch a saint,
With saints dost bait thy hook! Most dangerous
Is that temptation that doth goad us on
To sin in loving virtue.

(II.ii. 171–83)

There is a vicious circle here, since the saintlier Isabella is, the more Angelo will desire her. So any sincere refusal from her would only arouse him still further. Yet Isabella's searing refusal to lay down the treasure of her body to Angelo is charged with an erotic power that might well evoke a gleam in the eye of the most depraved marquis in the audience, to say nothing of a saint-turned-sensualist like Angelo:

were I under the terms of death,
Th' impression of *keen whips* I'd wear as rubies,
And *strip myself* to death *as to a bed,*
That longing have been sick for, ere I'd *yield*
My body up to shame.

(II.iv. 100–4, my italics)

In its dramatic context, this speech is peculiarly powerful. Other Shakespearian characters (such as Claudio and Antony) associate death with sex; and other threatened heroines of the time (e.g. Jonson's Celia and Shakespeare's Lucrece) prefer torture or death to dishonour. But here and only here—or so a lurid play-bill might put it—are fused the red and black extremes of passion and pain, the agonies and ecstacies of desire and martyrdom, of repression and sensuality (obviously, no commercially minded producer would dream of cutting this speech). Everything in it is associated with death, yet Isabella's fiery lines, with images of passionate sexuality underlying a prayer for martyrdom, for torture or death, for anything *but* sexual violation, would seem deliberately designed by Shakespeare to arouse Angelo as saint, as sensualist and as a sadist. And so, of

course, they do. Here is Angelo's response, his answer, his
ultimatum to Isabella:

> Angelo   I have begun,
> And now I give my sensual race the rein:
> Fit thy consent to my *sharp* appetite;
> *Lay by* all nicety and prolixious blushes
> *That banish what they sue for*; redeem thy
>   brother
> By *yielding up thy body* to my will;
> Or else he must not only die the death,
> But thy unkindness shall his death draw out
> To ling'ring sufferance.
>
>   (II.iv. 159–67)

Angelo seems to be recalling, and either deliberately or
unconsciously echoing, Isabella's memory-searing lines (her
speech comes less than five minutes playing-time before
his). She must fit her consent to his 'sharp appetite' (his
sexual equivalent of 'keen whips'?). She must 'lay by' (strip
herself of) all blushes 'That banish what they sue for'. In
short, she must come to *his* bed 'as to a bed/That longing
have been sick for' (there is surely a verbal echo in the
parallel phrases here). Otherwise, he will have Claudio
subjected to prolonged torture, before he has him killed.
    Angelo's lines are more explicitly sexual, his threats far
more sadistic, than earlier propositions urging Isabella to
ransom her brother with the treasure of her body. They are
also far more demanding. He insists upon a completely
uninhibited response, *however* unwilling Isabella is to give it.
This is what Coleridge saw as 'horrible'. Seeing sadism and
criminal sexuality in him, it was impossible for Coleridge to
accept the pardon and marriage of Angelo in Act 5: 'For
cruelty, with lust and damnable baseness, cannot be
forgiven, because we cannot conceive of them as being
morally repented of'. Whatever Shakespeare might wish
him to do at the end of a play so obviously concerned with

Christian forgiveness, Coleridge agreed with Dr Johnson (who was, likewise, a devout Christian as well as a great critic) that 'every reader feels some indignation when he finds [Angelo] spared'. It has been argued (see Kirsch 1975) that no such uncharitable and fundamentally un-Christian indignation would have been felt by Shakespeare's original audience. Elizabethan Christians (Kirsch asserts) would have rejoiced in the pardon and marriage of Angelo, whose 'libidinousness' was miraculously transformed by the bed-trick. Yet some Elizabethans might have agreed with Coleridge's conclusion that the ending 'baffles the strong indignant claim of justice' in so far as

> Faults should be measured by desart, but all is one in
> this,
> The lecher fyerd with lust, is punished no more,
> Than he which fel through force of loue, whose
> mariage salues his sore.
> (George Whetstone, *Promos and Cassandra*, 1578)

These (and other) lines from one of Shakespeare's major sources for *Measure for Measure*, would appear to suggest that ubiquitous mercy might have seemed, to individual Elizabethans, in *certain* circumstances, to be as unjust as ubiquitous justice seemed merciless. See *Promos and Cassandra*, Part 1, Act 2 (reprinted in Eccles 1980, pp. 313–15), where Isabella's counterpart thus pleads the case for Claudio's counterpart:

> Behold the wofull Syster here, of poor *Andrugio*,
> Whom though that lawe awardeth death, yet mercy do
> him show:
> Way [Weigh] his yong yeares, the force of love, which
> forced his amis,
> Way, way that Mariage, works amends, for what
> committed is,

He hath defilde no nuptial bed, nor forced rape hath
    mou'd,
He fel through love, who neuer ment, but wiue the
    wight he lou'd.
And wantons sure, to keepe in awe, these statutes first
    were made,
On none but lustfull leachers, should, with rygrous
    law be payd.
. . . .
Here is no wylful murder wrought, which axeth blood
    againe,
Andrugio's faulte may salued be, Mariage wipes out his
    stayne.

If, in the case of ubiquitous justice, we would all be denied
mercy ('Why, all the souls that were were forfeit once'), in
the case of ubiquitous mercy the claims of temporal justice
are unsatisfied, when (for instance) a lecher fired with lust to
attempted blackmail, rape and murder, is 'punished no
more' than he 'which fel through force of loue, whose
mariage salues his sore'. There may (on the one hand) be
more rejoicing in heaven, or at the end of a tragi-comedy like
Measure for Measure (or *Promos and Cassandra*), when sins
that were as scarlet are washed as white as snow. But, on a
temporal level, where 'Faults should be measured by
desart', the rejoicing may be tempered by a recognition that
this process baffles the strong indignant claims of justice (see
Ch. 2).

Looked back at from a different perspective,
Shakespeare's original portrayals of Angelo and Isabella in
their great confrontation scenes make the subsequent action
of the play seem frustrating in another way. When Angelo's
ultimatum is viewed from a psychological angle, it appears
obvious that he sees in Isabella the feminine counterpart of
himself (see Rossiter 1961, p. 159). As he was, so she is; as he
is, so she might become. As 'black masks/Proclaim an
enshielded beauty ten times louder/Than beauty could,

display'd' (II.iv. 79–81), so the saintly asceticism of her life, precisely like his own, may mask a keen appetite that could indeed give full and fit consent to his desire. As he will give the 'sensual race the rein', so must she: he will allow her no modesty, no nicety, no blushes to banish what he now believes they sue for. He will have a response equivalent to his own sexual passion. Could Angelo be right in attributing to Isabella a latent sensuality equal to his own? Does the fact that Angelo once believed himself immune to sex and now is obsessed with it, suggest that Isabella might fall too? Claudio has informed us that

> As surfeit is the father of much fast,
> So every scope by the immoderate use
> Turns to restraint.
>
> (I.ii. 120–2)

So might not the reverse prove true for his sister, as for Angelo? Could her restraint turn to immoderate use? Does her initial desire for more severe restraints within the convent suggest that there is something to restrain? Why does Isabella embrace martyrdom in such passionately sexual terms? Unless the line between saint and sinner, martyr and masochist, righteous severity and sadism—in short, the borderline between angelic and demonic extremes of virtue and of vice—is indeed a very narrow one and all too easy to cross? One may relish or deplore the psychological and sexual reverberations of Shakespeare's confrontations between a fiery saint and a fallen angel, but who would not be fascinated by them? 'Where's that palace whereinto foul things sometimes intrude not?' In the audience? On the stage? Why do Isabella's last lines in the play stress Angelo's desire for her?

It could be that, in their confrontation scenes—before Mariana's name is ever mentioned—Shakespeare establishes mysterious and powerful psychological and sexual affinities between Angelo and Isabella that make the

bland domestic futures assigned them by the Duke seem
incredible, if not unacceptable, to some members of the
audience. If this play, in effect, transforms the audience
from witnesses to participants in its tragi-comic rituals, we
may emotionally participate in a kind of firelight flamenco
dance between comedy and tragedy, piety and impiety,
virtue and vice, wherein one may threaten, arouse, change
places with, embrace—or, finally, repel—the other. For at
mid-point in the action (immediately following the major
confrontation scenes), there is a dramatic and virtually
complete withdrawal of attention from the sexual and
psychological proclivities of Shakespeare's heroine and his
villain. He never again permits them a moment alone
together on the stage. And so he abruptly and
conspicuously parts company with his sources (see Lever
1945, pp. xxxv–lv) wherein the counterpart to Isabella
always yields her body up, for one night, to Angelo's
counterpart. But, then, in none of the sources is the heroine
a young novice, nor is the sexual and emotional situation
anything like so highly charged. Perhaps for these reasons
Shakespeare summons forth the lovelorn Mariana to play
the bed-trick, thus assuring that Angelo will be securely
fettered to another woman by the bonds of holy wedlock,
and then (ever widening the safety-zone between his
incendiary pair) he has the Duke claim Isabella for his own.
Yet Angelo himself asks only for death—never for
Mariana—while Isabella's response to the Duke's proposal
is silence. And so, in the end, as in their confrontation
scenes, they still somehow seem, oddly, to be two of a kind.

　　Moreover, something more than Isabella's vanity may be
involved in her last reference to Angelo:

　　　I partly think
A due sincerity govern'd his deeds
Till he did look on me.

(V.i. 443–5)

This could be a statement of dramatic fact, so far as the audience's verdict on Angelo is concerned. For the experience of watching an Angelo previously unmoved and invulnerable to temptation become obsessed by a young novice makes its dramatic impression on the audience before the Duke informs us of Mariana's existence. In ways comparable to the doom of Pentheus by Dionysus, it is through Angelo's great soliloquies that Shakespeare most dramatically portrays the fall of a man who has never before known or felt desire. The subsequent information about Angelo's old contracting, and the succession of intrigues based on it may, therefore, seem perfunctorily contrived. Likewise, whether we approve of extreme asceticism or not, the passion for chastity which Isabella expressed with such uncompromising conviction in the confrontation scenes makes it difficult for certain people to believe that the same woman would willingly become the bride of anyone but Christ: 'Get her to a nunnery', one student exclaimed. As Mary Lascelles observes, it is easy to argue that it is 'the very idleness of criticism to ask how this play's new-married couples will settle down together' (Lascelles 1953, p. 137), and it is certainly true that Shakespeare frequently ends his comedies with matches which no marriage counsellor would sanction. Yet none of the parties to his other matches (with the noteworthy exception of Lucio) are characters originally endowed with personalities that seem so fundamentally hostile to the wedding-bells that toll for them, as Isabella and Angelo, who neither freely choose, nor verbally assent to, their domestic destinies. Of course you could, contrariwise, argue that they will be better off wed, even as F. R. Leavis insists that we should 'let Angelo marry a good woman and be happy' (Leavis 1952, p. 172), while W. W. Lawrence does not believe that 'there is any doubt that Isabella turns to [the Duke] with a heavenly and yielding smile' (Lawrence 1931, pp. 106–7). But the choice of responses (a smile, uncertainty, shock, joy, despair, resignation, etc.) is left open to the actress playing Isabella, and the actor playing Angelo, even as the individual members of the audience are free to respond to the characters, and their destinies, in altogether different ways.

Yet, however one looks at Shakespeare's original portrayals of Angelo and Isabella, as J. C. Maxwell has observed, it is easy to see the germs of twentieth-century psychological theories in the play: 'I have even been told of untutored playgoers who thought that it was Jonathan Miller and not Shakespeare who conceived the notion of setting it in [Freud's city] Vienna' (Maxwell 1974, p. 3). For that matter, *Measure for Measure* has recently been subjected to what, to my mind, may be the most inane of all the Freudian interpretations currently being imposed upon Shakespeare's plays. For instance, several critics have felt obliged to inform us that Claudio's fear of death can be interpreted, 'in Freudian terms', as a fear of 'castration' (see Garber 1980, p. 123, and Berry 1981, p. 51). But if so, then what of it? Critically speaking, this would seem on all fours with arguing that a fear of the diagnosis 'syphilis' ultimately accounts for a young patient's response to the diagnosis 'It's terminal cancer'. All one need do is glance back at Claudio's own account of all that men—and women—have feared of death itself (see p. 15 above) to realise what is lost by making Freudian trifles of Shakespearian terrors: the threat to 'splay and geld all the young men in the city' (II.i. 218) is not the one that Claudio faces here. Moreover, if 'fear of castration' or 'symbolic castration' constitutes a psychoanalytical metaphor for a fear of, or a loss of, identity; of integrity; of potency; of face; of life itself; then it cannot, simultaneously, serve to account for the phenomena it was devised to describe: 'Even in the analyst's office there is little room for diagnoses like the ones offered as psychoanalysis of characters—a psychoanalytic tag offered as an explanation, as though the name made the behaviour any more explicable' (Skura 1981, pp. 38–42). Some Freudian interpretations of *Measure for Measure* are admittedly, albeit unintentionally, hilarious. What about, say, the costuming, headgear, etc., required to put this one on the stage?

> [In the Fifth Act] the Duke's penetration of the city limits, the opening gates, the holy fountain a league below, all contribute to a powerfully sexual atmosphere. His homecoming is metaphorically portrayed in terms of a vaginal penetration.
>
> (Sacks 1980, p. 59)

What the play we actually have would seem to demonstrate is that Freud was by no means the first to have recognised the existence of subconscious desires, or to have noted that sexual repression can result in neurosis, in a diseased imagination, in psycho-sexual aberrations. All this appears to have been just as obvious to Shakespeare, as well as his near-contemporary Robert Burton, as it is to a student of Freud. Indeed, Robert Burton's compendium of Renaissance psychological theories, *The Anatomy of Melancholy*, can provide us with external evidence, if any is needed, that certain sexual, social and emotional problems posed in *Measure for Measure* are no more amenable to solution-by-diagnosis in Freudian terms than they were amenable to a single theological or social or political solution-by-diagnosis in Shakespeare's (or in any other) time.

In his discussions of sexual and religious pathology, Burton (very like Shakespeare in *Measure for Measure*) brings together 'Great precisians' (like Angelo) and 'fiery-spirited zealots' (like Isabella), as well as certain types that may well have composed a large part of Shakespeare's audience, as of his *dramatis personae*: there are the 'good, bad, indifferent, true, false, zealous, ambidexters, neutralists, lukewarm, libertines, atheists, etc.' (Burton 1932, iii, p. 387). In Burton, as in Shakespeare, virtue itself may turn into vice: 'howsoever they may seem to be discreet', the 'preposterous zeal' of great precisians (like Angelo) may result in actions that go 'beyond measure' (iii,

p. 372). In sexual matters, 'Venus omitted' may do just as
much damage as 'intemperate Venus'—it may cause
'priapismus, satyriasis, etc.' and 'send up poisonous
vapours to the brain and heart'. If the 'natural seed be over-
long kept (in some parties) it turns to poison' (i, p. 234). To
Burton, the tyranny of religious 'superstition' seemed as
terrible as the tyranny of princes: 'What power of prince or
penal law, be it never so strict', could enforce men and
women (rather like Isabella) to do that which they will
voluntarily undergo out of religious fervour: 'As to fast
from all flesh, abstain from marriage ... whip themselves ...
abandon the world?' (iii, p. 332). Religious and ideological
zealots of this kind will endure any misery, 'suffer and do
that which the sunbeams will not endure to see, *religionis acti
furiis*'; 'endure all extremities', 'vow chastity', 'take any
pains', 'die a thousand deaths' (iii, p. 350).

According to Burton, organised religion itself may
provide dispensations that are spurious, ways out that are
too easy. As a Protestant, Burton deplored the 'general
pardons' issued by Catholics, and complained that their
'ghostly fathers' all too easily 'apply remedies ... cunningly
string and unstring, wind and unwind their devotions, play
upon their consciences with plausible speeches and terrible
threats, ... settle and remove, erect with such facility and
deject, let in and out' (iii, pp. 403–4). I have never seen,
anywhere, what appears to be a better gloss on the dubious
contrivances of Shakespeare's Duke-disguised-as-a-friar, as
he plays upon the consciences of the other characters; sets
up, and then removes, the rod of law; arbitrarily orders
people into, and out of, death-row; and finally issues general
pardons for all offences. One could, using Burton's
arguments, write an essay concluding that Shakespeare
himself intended us to be comparably critical of the Duke.
But it is just as easy to argue the opposite case: given the
structure of the play, Shakespeare appears to be on the side
of the Duke, whose compromises, contrivances,
improvisations, and intrigues may be necessary in order to

maintain any semblance of stability or order or justice or mercy in a fallen world (see Schleiner 1982). Yet markedly unlike the Duke, Shakespeare's play itself 'does not' (my terms are again from Burton) 'repeal a fornicator' (like Julietta), 'reject a drunkard' (like Barnardine) or 'resist a proud fellow' (like Lucio), but 'entertains all, communicates itself to all (iii, p. 413). It is in this spacious humanity that Shakespeare himself might be said to reflect the amazing grace of God. Yet he also pays dramatic tribute to 'the devil's burning throne', and the falling, fallen, Angelo stands among the greatest of all his creations.

For here as elsewhere, Shakespeare was not about to subordinate his apprehension of a most protean reality to the dictates of any single dogma, doctrine or dramatic form. Thus the order superimposed on the play in the end is challenged by the recalcitrance of certain characters (like Lucio) even as the Duke's order, 'Love her, Angelo', raises questions as to whether affections can be so ordered.

> To interpose a jurisdictive power upon the inward and irremediable disposition of man, to command love and sympathy, to forbid dislike ... is not within the province of any law to reach.
>
> In whom therefore either the will, or the faculty is found to have never joined, or now not to continue so, 'tis not to say, they shall be one flesh, for they cannot be one flesh [though wedlock try all her golden links, and borrow to her aid all the iron manacles and fetters of law, it does but seek to twist a rope of sand].
> (Milton, ed. Sirluck, 1959, pp. 346, 606; the interpolation is from p. 345)

So far as the 'inward and irremediable disposition of man' is concerned, you can whip a Lucio, or force him to marry the whore he got with child, but short of hanging him, there's no way to stifle his jeers at all authority. You can pull down all the brothels in the suburbs, but the trade will only move elsewhere, and the brothels in the city that some 'wise burgher put in for' will still stand (I.ii. 91–102): the pimp will not be 'whipt out of his trade' (II.i. 242). Yet commercial prostitution here seems relatively innocuous when compared to Angelo's 'salt appetite' and 'sharp imagination' that desires to raze the sanctuary and pitch its evils there: 'For out of the heart proceed evil thoughts, murders, adulteries, fornications, thefts, false witness ... These are the things which defile a man.'

And so Shakespeare provokes speculation about the ways of an imaginary world (not altogether unlike our own) wherein 'Some rise by sin, and some by virtue fall' (II.i. 38), and the same individual may 'become much more the better/For being a little bad' (V.i. 438–9), and the same thing may 'make bad good, and good provoke to harm' (IV.i. 15). Included among the creatures who inhabit it are spiders and flies, burrs that stick, the basest of weeds, and lilies that fester. In this teeming terrain—and not in an ending which appears to have tidied everything up—may lie the source of the play's vitality, of its enduring relevance. To my mind anyway, what seem least significant about *Measure for Measure*, and certain critical interpretations of it, are the solutions officially offered us, whereby 'all difficulties are but easy when they are known' (IV.ii. 192–3) and all its moral, sexual, psychological conundrums can be resolved through substitutions, bed-tricks and marriage certificates. What seem most significant are the open questions posed throughout the play.

For the fact is that, whether Shakespeare intended them to or not, the *kinds* of solutions to the problems offered to us at the end of *Measure for Measure* seem obviously inadequate in the face of the psychological, social, sexual and moral conflicts they are supposed to have resolved. By contrast, it seems just fine when, for instance, certain problems posed in the beginning of *The Comedy of Errors* are solved when twin finally meets twin, and Aegeon is spared.

For the death-threat to Aegeon was, from the outset, amenable to a practical solution (i.e. the payment of 1,000 marks), even as the dramatic complications arising from the mistaking of one twin for another can, instantaneously, be unravelled when both twins finally appear together on the stage.

Count Otto von Bismarck described politics as 'the art of the possible', and Sir Peter Medawar has described scientific research as 'the art of the soluble', and both these descriptions could be applied to a certain kind of dramatic art, in which the playwright poses problems, however complicated they may appear to be, that are finally amenable to a dramatic resolution. On the other hand, a very different kind of dramatic art operates at certain crucial points in *Measure for Measure*, and it might be most accurately described as the 'art of the *insoluble*'. Perhaps a quick account of the way *Measure for Measure* differs from John Marston's *The Malcontent* can illustrate the differences between the two kinds of dramatic art.

It is obvious at a glance that the general outlines of *Measure for Measure* and *The Malcontent* are similar. Within the corrupt societies of both plays, a disguised duke manipulates characters and intrigues so that the outcome of a play which might otherwise have developed in the pattern of revenge tragedy results in mercy and harmony. Here the similarity ends, and some illuminating differences emerge. Where the ending of *Measure for Measure* creates difficulties, the conclusion of *The Malcontent* leaves the audience satisfied, or at least comparatively few commentators have objected to the way the conflicts are resolved. Where Marston's characterisation and style are consistent, the characters, the language and the action of Shakespeare's play sometimes appear at odds with each other. Marston's characters pose no insoluble problems for anyone familiar with Elizabethan drama.

His disguised Duke, Altofronto, speaking as Malevole, sounds enough like Jonson's Macilente and other characters of the same type to be readily accepted as the play's satiric spokesman from the moment he opens his mouth. The villainous usurper Mendoza is a nicely portrayed Machiavel with a Marlovian flair for overstatement; and the other characters need no more detailed introduction to any audience or reader even superficially familiar with their dramatic predecessors and contemporaries. We have Celso, the loyal friend and confidante; Bilioso, the doddering old man; various licentious courtiers; a virtuous duchess; a fool; a bawd. However bitter Marston's portrayal of this upside-down world may be, its inhabitants are old dramatic friends whose ancestors, siblings and progeny people many of the most popular plays on the Elizabethan stage. We know exactly what to expect from them, and they live up to our expectations (in the manner of Jonson's 'humour' types). All Marston has to do, given his skilful depiction of these well-known types, is to set them in action in a series of interesting intrigues. And his characters are such conventionally theatrical figures, that even when the action moves in an ominous direction, nobody in the audience really worries. The highly theatrical posturing, running about, double murder assignments and masque are great fun to watch. Marston's world is certainly out of joint, but it is so obviously a theatrically disordered world that there is no surprise when the playwright—via his spokesman and agent, Malevole/Altofronto—manages, theatrically, to set it right. For any problems created by the dramatic intrigues of one set of characters may be effectively solved by the dramatic intrigues of another group of characters, even as dramatic 'humours' can be dramatically expelled. In the *Prologue*, Marston stresses the lively action of the play, and rightly describes it as a comedy, since, however dark and devious his dramatic world may be, the emphasis falls on the dramatic intrigues, not on the suffering, which it causes.

By contrast, the action of *Measure for Measure* involves extreme suffering, and if Shakespeare exaggerates the traits of certain characters, he does so in ways significantly different from Marston's stylised exaggeration. Where Marston anchors his characters and action in the dramatic tradition, Shakespeare looses our dramatic moorings at the same time that he disturbs familiar ethical and moral assumptions. For instance, morally speaking, Barnardine is awful ('Unfit to live or die': IV.iii. 60). But Shakespeare's drunken, impenitent murderer, this death-defying, Duke-defying, 'careless', 'reckless', 'fearless', 'insensible' and 'desperately mortal' jailbird elicits an emotional and imaginative approbation that transcends critical and moral and ducal judgements alike. 'Whether the qualities that have made [Barnardine] deathless in the imagination of many readers were part of Shakespeare's design, or came from that bounty which he could hardly deny any of his creatures—here lies no certainty, nor the hope of any' (Lascelles 1953, p.113). No one writes that way about any *minor* character in *The Malcontent*. The same holds true for the major characters.

Where Marston gives us old dramatic acquaintances, Shakespeare gives us characters different from the *dramatis personae* in his own works or in those of his contemporaries. There are numerous Elizabethan and Jacobean villains like Marston's Mendoza, and there are plenty of pure heroines like his Maria. There are none like Angelo or Isabella. Until III.i. 153, Angelo, Isabella, and Claudio (when he faces death) behave with the intensity of tragic protagonists, as if they were impelled by elemental forces (the force of Eros, the will-to-autonomy, the will-to-live) and so are capable of surprising and shocking the audience, each other, themselves. All three are associated with absolutes. Angelo is absolute for the letter of the law, then for Isabella. Isabella is absolute for chastity. Claudio soon becomes absolute for life. And an audience that has witnessed their confrontations is left, not with a vague impression, but with an absolute conviction that, given their situations, each would choose to bring tragic suffering upon each other, themselves, etc., that Angelo would, without doubt, defile

Isabella in spite of his own horrified conscience; that Isabella would never yield to Angelo, even to save her brother's life; that Claudio could not willingly choose death, even to save his sister from a fate worse than death.

Thus, on the one hand, Shakespeare creates a desire to watch these characters face the tragic truths and consequences of their own decisions and desires and, on the other hand, creates a counter-desire to see how he—or the Duke—is going to save them from death, dishonour, each other, themselves, and so on. So far as dramatic form is concerned, Kenneth Burke has described the ways differing forms of dramatic art create, and satisfy, differing appetites, needs and desires on the part of the audience (Burke 1964, pp. 20–33). Shakespearian comedy can satisfy us like a wish-fulfilment dream, wherein all losses are restored and sorrows end; tragedy can satisfy a desire to go all the way, to see its characters confront the worst consequences of various passions and actions. *Measure for Measure* can be generically classified as a tragi-comedy since it creates, and attempts to satisfy, both desires. But in drama, as in life, the satisfaction of one desire may, necessarily, entail the frustration of the opposite desire. It may be impossible to arrive at a critical consensus about *Measure for Measure* because of the differing appetites it arouses, and satisfies, and frustrates, in differing individuals.

Measure for Measure can also be accurately described as a 'problem play' in so far as it confronts the audience, as well as its characters, with conflicts that are no more amenable to a final solution in art, or, for that matter, to critical resolution, than they are amenable to a final solution in real life. In the next chapter I shall argue that among such conflicts are the ones between a temporal necessity (and desire) for justice, to judge, to see the law impartially enforced, and a counter-necessity (and desire) for mercy: 'Forgive your enemies.' 'Judge not that ye be not judged.'

· 2 ·

'On the other hand'
Justice and Mercy in
'Measure for Measure'

An audience would hardly see virtue in a man who
insisted on sending a youth to death for a venial offence,
in the face of moving appeals for mercy uttered by a
beautiful heroine.

(W. W. Lawrence, *Shakespeare's Problem Comedies*)

For suppose condemnation to follow these present
proceedings. Would it be so much we ourselves that
would condemn as it would be martial law operating
through us? For that law and the rigour of it, we are not
responsible.... But the exceptional in the matter moves
the hearts within you. Even so too is mine moved. But let
not warm hearts betray heads that should be cool. Ashore
in a criminal case will be an upright judge allow himself
off the bench to be waylaid by some tender kinswoman of
the accused seeking to touch him with her tearful plea?

(Captain Vere in Melville's *Billy Budd*)

Isabella　　　　　How would you be
If He, which is the top of judgment, should
But judge you as you are? O think on that;
And mercy then will breathe within your lips,
Like man new made.

43

Angelo   Be you content, fair maid.
It is the law, not I condemn your brother.
Were he my kinsman, brother, or my son,
It should be thus with him.

(*Measure for Measure*, II.ii. 75–82)

Some Conflicting Judgements

In an essay on 'The Renaissance Background of *Measure for Measure*' (*Shakespeare Survey* 2 (1949), p. 74), Elizabeth M. Pope quotes a contemporary distinction between two kinds of equally bad judges. The first kind are 'such men, as by a certain kind of pity are so carried away that [they] would have nothing but *mercy, mercy* and would ... have the extremity of the law executed on no man. This is the high way to abolish laws, and consequently to pull down authority, and so in the end to open a door to all confusion, disorder, and to all licentiousness of life.' The second kind are

> such men as have nothing in their mouths, but the *law*, the *law*; and *Justice, Justice*; in the meantime forgetting that Justice always shakes hands with her sister mercy, and that all laws allow a mitigation.... These men, therefore, strike so precisely on their points, and the very tricks and trifles of the law, as (so the law be kept, and that in the very extremity of it) they care not, though equity were trodden under foot.

There would, ideally, appear to be a middle ground, where mercy seasons justice, and this would seem to be the ideal finally realised by the Duke in Act 5 of *Measure for Measure*. The criminals all get a measure of mercy, as well as a measure of justice. Angelo has done unto him what he wanted to do to Isabella (and so is consigned to the bed of

someone he did not choose to have intercourse with) even as
he is ordered to remedy the wrong he did to Mariana—
'Look that you love your wife'—but he is spared the death
penalty that he asks for in his last lines of the play:
'Immediate sentence then and sequent death/Is all the grace I
beg' ... 'I crave death more willingly than mercy;/'Tis my
deserving, and I do entreat it.' Lucio is spared whipping and
hanging, but he is forced to marry the woman who bore his
child:

Lucio	Marrying a punk, my lord, is pressing to death, whipping, and hanging.
Duke	Slandering a prince deserves it.

Barnadine is spared the death sentence for murder, but is
assigned to the custody of a friar to learn better how to live.
Claudio is pardoned, but is told to right whatever 'wrong'
he did to Julietta; 'She, Claudio, that you wrong'd, look you
restore.' Thus one could argue that the Duke's pardons and
sentences simultaneously satisfy and reconcile the claims of
justice, equity and mercy. Angelo, Joseph Summers
concludes, surely 'deserves to have the bed-trick played on
him if anyone ever did; perhaps only after such a trick (with
his lustful imagination and pretensions to villainy as
thoroughly humbled as his sanctimonious image and
pretensions to authority) could we find him forgivable'
(Summers 1984, p.81). Yet there are also good reasons why
other people have, on the one hand, felt that the ending
baffles the strong, indignant claims of justice and, on the
other hand, complained that the quality of mercy here
extended seems strained to the breaking-point.

The comparative willingness, or unwillingness, of
Claudio, Angelo and Lucio to marry Julietta, Mariana and
Kate Keepdown, respectively, would seem to be the only
thing that differentiates between their sentences. Lucio goes,
protesting, to marry his punk. Angelo and Claudio are

silent. But whereas Claudio always wanted to marry Julietta ('she is fast my wife'), Angelo would seem to 'crave death more willingly than mercy' as embodied in the form of Mariana. But has his response changed (to joy, to love) when he finally leaves the stage as a married man? I realise there may be textual omissions in the final scene (see Watts 1986, p. 77), but Angelo's last lines in the play as it stands plead for justice, for consequences, for death. In no other Shakespearian comedy are so *many* characters (e.g. Angelo, Isabella, Julietta, Claudio and Barnardine) so silent (silenced?) at the very end. And in no other major Elizabethan play does the way comic closure is achieved so much depend on the way silences are interpreted by the individual actors on-stage or by the reader off-stage. Contrast, for instance, the way the fickle Demetrius (in *A Midsummer-Night's Dream*) as it were officially announces to the audience that his desire for Hermia was a false appetite compared to his true love for Helena; the magical intervention of Oberon has thus assured that Helena will live happily ever after with the eternally enchanted Demetrius. Likewise, Bertram (in *All's Well That Ends Well*) personally, albeit feebly, proclaims to us that he will, henceforth, love his Helena 'ever, ever dearly'. But Angelo says nothing of the kind about Mariana. We might feel differently about Lucio's future if, like the character tricked into marrying a witty whore in Middleton's *A Chaste Maid in Cheapside*, he, himself, had finally decided to embrace and make the best of his comic destiny. One could, of course, argue that marriage is (or was, to Shakespeare) the one and only theological, social, moral and dramatic way of controlling, sanctioning and finally sanctifying the sexual acts involved in *Measure for Measure*. Yet it would seem, to say the least, a let-down, if 'every girl should be married' were the ultimate message delivered to us by its author. For that matter, there are obvious reasons why some people have felt that some of the measures here resorted to in order to achieve that end (like the bed-trick) are essentially, if not historically or intentionally (Shakespeare consistently portrays Mariana in sympathetic terms), as humiliating and degrading to the women involved as they are to the men. For instance, as Carol Thomas Neely has observed, 'Angelo experiences the satisfaction of his aggressive lust solely as a degradation of Isabella and himself':

> A deflow'red maid!
> And by an eminent body that enforc'd
> The law against it!
>
> (IV.iv. 19–21)

'At the denouement, both [Isabella and Mariana] testify explicitly of their shameful enforced compliance in a fictional or actual sexual encounter—in rape. Isabella describes giving the "gift of my chaste body/To his concupisable, intemperate lust" (V.i. 97–8), and Mariana chillingly attests to Angelo that her body "did supply thee at thy garden-house" (V.i. 212)' (Neely 1985, p. 95). One could also argue that there is a sense in which the Duke's coercive, authoritarian manipulation of the women involved in the bed-trick seems comparable to his setting-up of Angelo:

> The maid will *I* frame and make fit for *his* attempt.
>
> (III.i. 248, my italics)

How holy are the wedlocks resulting from such measures? With Angelo, the script's emphasis is on the sexual desires that trapped him into marriage with a woman for whom he never expresses any affection (see Novy 1984, pp. 15–16). At the end of *Measure for Measure*, Mariana and Angelo do not work out their marriage for themselves; it is effected by ducal fiat: 'Go, take her hence and marry her instantly' (V.i. 375).

'We ourselves esteem not of that obedience, or love, or gift which is of force', wrote Milton: 'God commands not impossibilities; and all the ecclesiastical glue, that liturgy, or laymen can compound is not able to solder up two such incongruous natures into the one flesh of a true beseeming marriage' (Milton 1959, p. 527 and p. 606). Although there is no legal difference between them, there is, nevertheless, all the difference in the world between a certificate symbolising the 'one flesh' of a 'true beseeming marriage' of two minds, which is freely subscribed to by both parties, and a piece of paper serving as a technical, cosmetic, face-saving device to legalise what would otherwise be deemed social/sexual shame/sin. And it seems especially sad when—or if—one party (say Mariana) signs the certificate as if it were the former, while the other party (say Angelo) signs it as if it were the latter.

Thus, depending on how the ending is read or staged, the very marriage that structurally clinches the comic resolution to *Measure for Measure* may bring to mind problems left unresolved on the psychological, emotional, level of action. Critically speaking, there are alternative ways to look at this phenomenon. You can (on the one hand) argue that the play is only a play; that the action is, after all, confined to the stage; that our off-stage response to it is dictated by the same dramatic conventions that determine the course of the action on stage; and thus the technical contrivances involved in the ending themselves assure that the audience will not confuse comic art with life. Or you can argue that marriage has, traditionally, albeit mistakenly, been deemed a kind of magical cure-all (compare the marriage of the heroine to the erstwhile villain in Richardson's *Pamela*). Or you can argue that this play's claim to greatness depends on the ways that it provokes (rather than shuts off) speculation about the characters and action, and arouses (rather than puts down) passionate responses, and so leaves the audience with what seems to be, and may in fact be, a new acquist of true experience that is more than literary, and which seems, somehow, both extra- and meta-dramatic. For instance, a class of mine once broke up because of the ferocity with which two students attacked *each other* in an argument about Isabella: 'You smug, damn, self-righteous prude!' 'You have no sense of moral or physical integrity yourself!' To the degree that *Measure for Measure* has, historically, and does, still, evoke passionately partisan responses (pro and con the differing characters, etc.) it seems pointless to argue that it does not, or should not, confuse life with art—and so infuse art with life—or that it is somehow *our* fault (e.g. our lack of critical sophistication or historical background) if it evokes extra-dramatic and extra-literary responses or speculations in us. For these may be the greatest of all its dramatic *virtues*.

But be that as it may, and however you look at the play, the differing measures of justice and mercy ultimately extended to Claudio, Lucio and Angelo alike depend on their—and our—positive, or negative, reactions to shot-gun weddings from which there is no appeal, no release, no escape. So far as enforced marriages are concerned, as A. D. Nuttall has observed, 'Elizabethan marriage held at its centre a high mystery', but 'at the same time it seems plain' that the ease with which it could be contracted or commanded had trivialised it: 'on the one hand we see old Capulet ... arranging a marriage for his daughter with a casual celerity which shocks us, and on the other marriage itself is so absolute' (Nuttall 1975, p. 56). For that matter, in the following Shakespearian catalogue of all the sources of woe in love and marriage alike, by far the most notable is the absence of mutuality; of freedom and 'sympathy in choice':

Hermia   O cross! too high to be enthrall'd to low.
Lysander Or else misgraffed in respect of years—
Hermia   O spite! too old to be engag'd to young.
Lysander Or else it stood upon the choice of friends—
Hermia   O hell! to choose love by another's eyes.
Lysander Or, if there were a sympathy in choice,
            War, death or sickness, did lay seige to it ...

(*A Midsummer-Night's Dream*, I.i. 136–42)

And there is no reason to presume that freedom and compatability of choice were somehow less important to Shakespeare's original audience than they are to us. According to Elizabethan law, the very basis for a *de praesenti* betrothal was, in fact, the mutual and 'free consent' of both parties (see Harding 1950, p. 144): 'It is to be knowen that man and woman dothe entre this holy ordre and sacramente of matrymony by expresse and free consente of both partyes ... and that consente doo shewe eyther to other by expresse wordes of the tyme presente.' For all we know to the contrary, Shakespeare may have had good (personal) reasons to feel ambivalent about shot-gun weddings; seeing them (on the one hand) as a matter of social necessity, yet, simultaneously, realising that the basis of a marriage of true minds is the mutual desire to give and receive love that, in turn, depends on the right to say 'no' when there is not 'a sympathy in choice'.

Whether there is a sense of redemption, of true happiness found or regained by the individual characters at the end of *Measure for Measure*, or (on the other hand) we are left with an awareness of the vast difference between the ideal of marriage and the sad reality of certain marriages, depends on the way the spaces between the lines of Shakespeare's script are interpreted by the individual reader or critic or director, or by the actors communicating the responses of the characters to the audience. The tragi-comic conventions of the play would seem to mandate a positive resolution, yet the resolution here achieved seems so forced as to evoke a negative reaction to it. Seeing characters choose virtue (or love or obedience or marriage or salvation) for themselves is one thing. Seeing salvation imposed upon them—like the Christian conversion forced upon Shylock—may have an altogether different effect, and in the script of *Measure for Measure* as it stands, Angelo, Lucio and Barnardine are not shown to have chosen, or to have achieved, virtue for themselves. They have virtue thrust upon them by the Duke. Thus the play may suggest that, while (or because) congenital vice (original sin?) cannot finally be expunged from the world, it can and must be controlled by temporal and spiritual authority (the Duke, the friar). But that message itself, like a shot-gun at a wedding, raises questions about the relative profundity, or superficiality, of the ultimate redemption, reformation and reconciliation of justice and mercy that is, or is not, or is only partially achieved, by his Grace the Duke.

Looked at dramaturgically, the life-sentences meted out to Lucio, Angelo and Barnardine bring us closer to the confinements ordered, in perpetuity, at the end of Ben Jonson's *Volpone* than to the kind of comic release involved at the end of, say, *The Tempest*. But in *Volpone* we watch a kind of dramatic automation go into effect whereby each step a character takes in a sequence of movements controls the next, so that we watch the knaves and fools themselves create their own dramatic destinies. By contrast, in *Measure for Measure*, the Duke imposes his own dramatic and moral designs upon the action. So, of course, does Prospero. But at the end of *The Tempest*, Prospero set everyone free to pursue their own destinies, for good or ill. In legal jargon, Prospero dismissed the jury and let the defendants go. Similarly, in Marston's *The Malcontent*, Duke Altofronto simply kicks out the villain and allows the other characters to pair off as they choose. By contrast, Duke Vincentio limits the freedom of his subjects to the incongruous futures he selects for them. Moreover, Prospero's 'rarer action' represented his personal pardon of traitors who had grievously injured him. Prospero himself has suffered, and we watch him struggle to forgive. But so far as the script of *Measure for Measure* is concerned, the worst thing that the Duke of Vienna appears to suffer from personally in his entire dramatic life, is a series of rather amusing, albeit scurrilous, slanders from Lucio, and the Duke finds Lucio's insults harder to pardon than any other offences in the play—major or minor, attempted or committed, including murder. And although this may be a brilliant stroke of

psychological realism on Shakespeare's part (see below,
p. 120), it does raise questions about the nature of the last
judgements issued in the play.

F. R. Leavis, among others, has argued that the Duke is a
'more than Prospero' whose 'total attitude' is the 'total
attitude of the play' (see Leavis 1952, pp. 163–9). And A. P.
Rossiter agrees with Leavis that 'what one makes of the
ending ... depends on what one makes of the Duke'. 'But',
Rossiter adds, 'I do not quite know what to make of the
Duke' (Rossiter 1961, p. 164). For the fact is that the play
itself offers us a choice between positive and negative
attitudes towards the Duke. For instance, in a most
significant departure from his sources (wherein the Duke's
counterpart is kept immaculately detached from the action
until he metes out justice and/or grants mercy in the end) in
Act 1, Scene 3 of *Measure for Measure*, Shakespeare
implicates his Duke by giving him three different reasons for
having invested Angelo with 'absolute power' and
ostensibly leaving Vienna, and all three of them would seem
to suggest that Shakespeare here holds the Duke himself to
account for the suffering experienced by, and inflicted upon,
his subjects.

1. The Duke has neglected to enforce the law for fourteen
   years, and the result is social chaos:

Duke   We have strict statutes and most biting laws,
        The needful bits and curbs to headstrong
                steeds,
        Which for these fourteen years we have let slip;
        . . . .
                                        so our decrees,
        Dead to infliction, to themselves are dead;
        And liberty plucks justice by the nose;

                                        (I.iii. 19–29)

2. He does not want to take the responsibility, or the rap,
   for enforcing the law ('Sith 'twas my fault to give the
   people scope'), and so has brought in Angelo to
   scourge the vice his own permissiveness had
   encouraged:

Friar   It rested in your Grace
        To unloose this tied-up justice when you
                pleas'd;
        And it in you more dreadful would have seem'd
        Than in Lord Angelo.
Duke   I do fear, too dreadful,
        Sith 'twas my fault to give the people scope,
        'Twould be my tyranny to strike and gall them
        For what I bid them do; for we bid this be done,
        When evil deeds have their permissive pass
        And not the punishment. Therefore, indeed,
                my father,
        I have on Angelo impos'd the office;
        Who may, in th' ambush of my name, strike
                home
        And yet my nature never in the fight
        To do in slander.
                                    (I.iii. 31–43)

3. He wants to test the icy Angelo for cracks in his facade:

        Moe reasons for this action
At our more leisure shall I render you.
Only, this one: Lord Angelo is precise;
Stands at a guard with envy; scarce confesses
That his blood flows, or that his appetite
Is more to bread than stone. Hence we shall see,
If power change purpose, what our seemers be.

                                    (I.iii. 48–54)

These differing motives make it hard to know how we are supposed to respond to the Duke. And his subsequent actions make it difficult to know how to interpret his original intentions. Or to whom to compare him (see Levin 1979, pp. 171–89, 212–13). Is he a Christlike figure of divine Grace, who ultimately extends mercy even unto the most grievous of sinners? Or does he hold a mirror for magistrates up to King James? Or does he reflect the activity of a writer of tragi-comedy, like Shakespeare himself? Are his political actions comparable to those of the great Caliph Haroun al Raschid—or the good Roman emperor, Alexander Severus—who mingled with the populace in disguise? Or is he like Ben Jonson's Emperor Tiberius, who gets Sejanus to do his political dirty work for him, and then destroys his deputy, even as Cesare Borgia destroyed Remirro de Orco (see p. 1 above)? In the cast list appended to *Sejanus* in the 1616 Folio of Jonson's *Works*, Richard Burbage heads the names in the first column, and 'Will. Shake-Speare' heads the names in the second column.

> Did [Burbage] play the title-part in *Sejanus*, and Shakespeare play Tiberius? In John Davies's *The Scourge of Folly*, 1610, Epigram 159 'To our English Terence Mr. Will. Shake-speare' there is a cryptic remark about his acting in royal parts:
>> Some say (good *Will*) which I, in sport, do sing,
>> Had'st thou not plaid some Kingly parts in sport,
>> Thou had'st bin a companion for a *King*;
>> And, beene a King among the meaner sort.
>
> (Herford and Simpson (eds), *The Works of Ben Jonson*, vol. 9, 1950, p. 262)

In suggesting that Shakespeare might have played Tiberius (p. 191) Herford and Simpson also note that 'Rowe first told us that Shakespeare played the Ghost' in *Hamlet* (first staged c1600). Given a connection between Shakespeare and comparably 'royal' parts, one cannot but wonder if, or how, he might have played the Emperor Tiberius (who is strongly associated with the power of 'fortune', as well as with the 'tyrant's arts' in *Sejanus* (1603)), and then played the Duke of Vienna, who is strongly associated with the powers of a playwright, as well as the temporal and metaphysical powers that be, in *Measure for Measure* (1604)—see also Muir 1979, p. 140, and Bennett 1966, pp. 135–7.

If Shakespeare played the Duke, this would lend an authorial dimension of meaning to certain lines ("tis an accident that Heaven provides'); and to the way the Duke, acting as surrogate playwright, takes charge of the action in order to effect a comic resolution; and to the ubiquitous pardons finally issued in the end, wherein the playwright would seem to be saying to his characters, 'Neither do I condemn thee: go, and sin no more'. It would also help to explain why Shakespeare dramatically implicates the Duke from the beginning: it is the *playwright* who is responsible for their predicaments, and who sets the traps that his characters fall into. For instance, to portray a character, like Angelo, who deems himself above temptation, is, dramatically, to set him up for his fall.

Perhaps significantly, Shakespeare makes it clear that Angelo, himself, did not seek the high office imposed upon him by the Duke. It is as if the playwright/Duke, in the course of his god-games, leads Angelo into temptation before he mercifully delivers him from evil:

Angelo   Now, good my lord,
          Let there be some more test made of my metal,
          Before so noble and so great a figure
          Be stamp't upon it.
Duke   No more evasion!
          We have with a leaven'd and prepared choice
          Proceeded to you.

                                        (I.i. 48–53)

By way of the action, Shakespeare raises the question
whether it is fair for the Duke to put a protesting Angelo to a
test for which he is unprepared (see Ornstein 1960, p. 257),
and then self-righteously condemn him for failing it—

> Twice treble shame on Angelo,
> To weed my vice and let his grow!
> O, what may man within him hide,
> Though angel on the outward side!
>
> (III.ii. 251–4)

—while conveniently forgetting, or ignoring, the fact that he
had deliberately appointed Angelo to confront a situation of
his own creation (i.e. to weed the vice he had let flourish in
Vienna) and so caused all the problems involved at the
outset, including Angelo's? Where is the justice in this?
'Who sins most?' (II.ii. 163), the tester or the tested, the
tempter or the tempted? 'Dost thou put upon me at once
both the office of God and the devil?' (*All's Well That Ends
Well*, V.ii. 46): the same question could be asked of the
Duke, by Angelo, and of Shakespeare by the Duke.

Did Angelo fall or was he pushed? 'Punish them to your
height of pleasure' says the Duke. Who, here, lets whose
vice grow? Moreover, if the Duke knew all along that
Angelo had wronged Mariana (III.i. 195–257), then he knew
at the outset that Angelo was not the paragon that he,
himself had seemed (?) to believe him to be when he officially
invested Angelo with his 'terror' and 'dress'd' him with his
'love' (I.i. 20–5). Why, then, cause unnecessary suffering for
a number of his subjects in order to find out what else might
lie behind Angelo's seeming sanctity? Like a tragic, or comic
playwright, or like a god, the Duke seems to believe that
what might, otherwise, appear to be unnecessary suffering
will prove instructive, or morally beneficial, to the parties
he inflicts it on. He does not, for instance, tell Isabella that
Claudio is alive, because he wants 'To make her heavenly
conforts of despair/When it is least expected' (IV.iii.

106–7). And he tells poor Claudio to abandon all hope of a reprieve. Then, godlike, he finally manifests his absolute power:

> *Angelo*   ... I perceive your Grace, like pow'r divine,
>   Hath look'd upon my passes.
>   (V.i. 367–8)

Throughout *Measure for Measure*, Angelo is portrayed as the subject, as well as the agent, of divine and demonic—as well as temporal—powers beyond his comprehension and control, even as the tragi-comedy in which he appears has certain obvious affinities with medieval religious drama. As in the mystery cycles, the god-of-the-action mingles with the lesser beings (the good and the bad, the true and the false, the libertines, blasphemers, fornicators, etc.) whom he finally judges. Like the figure of Mankind in a morality-play, Angelo is subject to conflicts between internal and external forces of Vice and of Virtue, besieged by temptations from the world, the flesh and the devil. But the differences between this play and its medieval precursors are even more significant than the similarities. In the case of the Duke, his roles as divine-power-and-grace-in-human-form, and as ultimate judge, do not involve any Christ-like suffering or sacrifice; indeed, Angelo serves as scapegoat for the Duke's past sins of omission (see Nuttall 1968, p. 246). Moreover, in medieval morality plays, Sanctity itself does not engender Vice, and there is never any question which is which, nor is there any doubt which is the Tempter—or 'Which is the wiser here, Justice or Iniquity?' (II.i. 163). In *Measure for Measure*, the reverse holds true, as it were with a vengeance: 'Let's write "good angel" on the devil's horn' (II.iv. 16).

> *Isabella* Save your honour!   [*exuent all but Angelo*]
> *Angelo*   From thee; even from thy virtue!
>   What's this, what's this? Is this her fault or
>   mine?

The tempter or the tempted, who sins most?
Ha!
Not she; nor doth she tempt; ...
. . . .
                              ...O, fie, fie, fie!
What dost thou, or what art thou, Angelo?
Dost thou desire her foully for those things
That make her good? ...
. . . .
O cunning enemy, that, to catch a saint,
With saints dost bait thy hook! Most
            dangerous
Is that temptation that doth goad us on
To sin in loving virtue. Never could the
            strumpet,
With all her double vigour, art and nature,
Once stir my temper; but this virtuous maid
Subdues me quite.   (II.iii. 161–86)

It is hard to think of a medieval morality-play wherein the
cunning enemy of mankind baits his hook with *Virtue*.

And so the complexities of the script itself make it
possible, on the one hand, to posit valid political and moral
arguments against the Duke, and, on the other hand, to
argue that Angelo can be seen, on a metaphysical as well as a
temporal level, as a victim as well as the villain of the play.
Moreover, Angelo's own virtue, his conscience, his
remorse, emerge in his agonised castigations of himself. The
ultimate punishment for Angelo's crimes may well be his
total, and irrevocable, loss (comparable to a loss of chastity
for an Isabella) of personal integrity and of all self-respect:

This deed unshapes me quite, makes me unpregnant
And dull to all proceedings. A deflow'red maid!
And by an eminent body that enforc'd
The law against it! But that her tender shame
Will not proclaim against her maiden loss,

How might she tongue me! ...
. . . .
                    ... He should have liv'd,
Save that his riotous youth, with dangerous sense,
Might in the times to come have ta'en revenge,
By so receiving a dishonour'd life
With ransom of such shame. Would yet he had liv'd!
Alack, when once our grace we have forgot,
Nothing goes right; we would, and we would not.
                                        (IV.iv. 18–32)

Indeed, Angelo's last lines in the play indicate that he,
finally, would prefer an immediate sentence of death to
'receiving a dishonour'd life/With ransom of such shame' as
his *own*.

By contrast, the Duke, who is described by Escalus as a
man who 'above all other strifes, contended especially to
know himself' (III.ii. 219) gives us no such soul-searching or
psychologically revealing soliloquies. Yet Leavis seems right
in associating the Duke with the 'total attitude of the play',
for he is the instigator, as well as the emergent god and judge
of the action within it, and our 'total attitude' towards, or
interpretation of, the play may ultimately depend on what
kind of god we judge him to be, and on whether we conclude
that his ways, as its *deus abscondicus* and *deus ex machina* are,
or are not, justified, or justifiable, to *us*. Looked at in one
way, the play develops a positive image of his Grace as the
dramatic embodiment of an ultimately benevolent
Providence, of a just, yet merciful, God. But that image itself
is developed from a negative image dramatically comparable
to this one:

O Thou, who didst with pitfall and with gin   [trap]
Beset the Road I was to wander in,
    Thou wilt not with Predestined Evil round
Enmesh, and then impute my Fall to Sin!
        (*The Rubáiyát of Omar Khayyám*, stanza 49)

Throughout *Measure for Measure*, Shakespeare associates
the Duke with metaphysical as well as temporal power, in
the countless lines addressed to, or descriptive of him, as
'My dread lord', 'O most bounteous sir', 'my most gracious
lord', 'good father', 'ghostly father', 'O my good lord',
'your Grace, like pow'r divine', 'Your unknown
sovereignty', 'my hidden pow'r', 'Grace of the Duke', 'your
royal grace', 'The old fantastical Duke of dark corners',
'greatness in mortality', 'heavenly comforts', many of which
suggest prayers to, or descriptions of, a 'dread' or 'gracious'
deity, as well as a Prince. For that matter, whether we like
him or not, the Duke's 'sword of heaven' speech (III.ii.
243–63) seems to some of us 'wonderfully strange and
efective ... distinguished by its power of compression and
its unusual rhythmic urgency' (Miles 1976, p.180). It is
unlike any other speech in *Measure for Measure*. Yet its
'unusual rhythmic urgency' is comparable, in incantational
power, with those spell-casting, spell-dissolving speeches
associated with supernatural forces in Shakespeare's
previous, and subsequent, works:

> Duke   He who the sword of heaven will bear
>   Should be as holy as severe;
>   Pattern in himself to know,
>   Grace to stand, and virtue go.
>
>   (see III.ii. 243ff)

> Oberon   Be as thou was wont to be;
>   See as thou was wont to see.
>   Dian's bud o'er Cupid's flower
>   Hath such force and blessed power.
>   (*A Midsummer-Night's Dream*, IV.i. 68–71)

> 1. *Witch*   When shall we three meet again?
>   In thunder, lightning, or in rain?
> 2. *Witch*   When the hurlyburly's done,
>   When the battle's lost and won.
>   (*Macbeth*, I.i. 1–4)

It is not surprising that critical responses to the Duke range a metaphysical and temporal spectrum from hosannas to hatred, from Escalus-like panegyrics to Lucio-like exposés of him as a 'fleshmonger, a fool, and a coward' (V.i. 331–2). After all, these are the responses that temporal power itself well-nigh inevitably evokes both on and off the stage:

> Duke   O place and greatness! Millions of false eyes
> Are struck upon thee. Volumes of report
> Run with these false, and most contrarious
>   quest
> Upon thy doings. Thousand escapes of wit
> Make thee the father of their idle dream
> And rack thee in their fancies.
>   (IV.i. 58–63)

And so does 'pow'r divine': 'I am made all things to all men' (1 Corinthians, 9:22).

As it were in critical reaction to the most extreme of critical reactions *pro* or *con* the Duke, certain recent arguments and productions seem devised to divest him of both our terror and our love, so as 'to make modern and familiar things supernatural and causeless' (*All's Well That Ends Well*, II.iii. 1–3). Yet it seems to me that critical conclusions whereby, on the one hand, the Duke is 'fallible, meddling and laughable', although, on the other hand, he is 'beneficent, inventive, and in large measure successful in helping his subjects' (see Schleiner 1982) tend to fall flat, to defuse and de-fang and diminish the play as well as the Duke. And in so far as they assume that we should adopt a patronising and condescending attitude towards all the characters in *Measure for Measure*, including the Duke, so have the performances I've seen wherein he appeared as a jolly good fellow, albeit a laughable meddler: all of them were flops. For whatever else the Duke is, he is one of the biggest acting parts in the complete works of Shakespeare, who (whichever ones he himself played) wrote the greatest parts in English drama for actors, and who, so far as I know, *never* minimises, but *maximises* the dramatic impacts and reverberations of a given part. How then, should the Duke be played?

In a telephone conversation-interview, I asked Robert Hardy (whom I've long wished to see as Angelo, and now would go miles to see play the Duke) about the technical difficulties involved for a actor. As evidence that the problems the Duke poses are not insoluble on the stage, Robert Hardy described Harry Andrews's performance as the Duke in the RSC production at Stratford-upon-Avon in 1950. Andrews spoke the Duke's oracular and expository lines in a 'curiously powerful way', creating a 'big character' from the outset, in which he acted as 'real Authority, true Authority' standing aside, then returning to take charge, 'as boss', with the formidable force 'and logic of a *deus ex machina*'. The actors debated whether Lucio knows who he is speaking to in those scurrilous lines directed to the 'old, fantastical Duke of dark corners' himself, and decided that he does not; but in either case, 'here is the *dramatist* himself insisting that the powers that act on, and expose us, are not pure—and we should not be surprised that they aren't.' Nor should the highest of all authorities be exempt from witty attack. The sinister side of the Duke was not played down by Andrews, nor was the good side. For in the script of *Measure for Measure* itself Shakespeare 'gives us the good and bad sides of *everything*, human and superhuman'. In the case of Angelo, Shakespeare has us look at the 'worst enemy, at what we most despise' with a kind of compassion and understanding: Angelo is a great part '*because* he faces enormous temptations of every kind'. Like every other part in *Measure for Measure*, the Duke should be played for maximum dramatic impact, and with maximum authority and sympathy on the part of the actor; and Shakespeare's script as it stands can be trusted to communicate its ambivalances to the audience. They are 'built-in' to the part.

Robert Hardy's conclusion that *Measure for Measure* gives the good and bad sides of 'everything human and superhuman' in it, seems to me dramatically confirmed by the script, and critically confirmed by the 'on the one hand ... on the other hand' rhetoric underlying countless discussions of the play, including this one. Indeed, that rhetoric itself may prove as critically and dramatically significant as it is scientifically interesting:

> Right hand, left hand, that was the deep clue that Pasteur followed in his study of life. The world is full of things whose right-hand version is different from its left-hand version: a right-handed corkscrew as against a left-handed, a right snail as against a left one. Above all, the two hands; they can be mirrored one in the other, but they cannot be turned in such a way that the right hand and left hand become interchangeable. That was known in Pasteur's time to be true also of some crystals whose facets are so arranged that there are right-hand versions and left-hand versions.... In his first piece of research he had hit on the notion that there must be right-handed and left-handed molecules too; and what is true of the crystal must reflect a property of the molecule itself.... We still do not know why life has this strange chemical property. But the property establishes that life has a specific chemical character, which has maintained itself throughout evolution. For the first time Pasteur had linked all the forms of life with one kind of chemical structure.
>
> (Bronowski 1973, p.313)

Pasteur's deep clue for the 'study of life' could serve as a description of Shakespeare's dramatic practice in *Measure for Measure*, or as an account of the deep-structure, the basic chemistry, of the tragi-comedy itself which determines the properties of the individual molecules that interact within it. For the world of the play is, likewise, 'full of things' (e.g. asceticism, sexuality, law, 'pow'r divine' etc.) whose 'right-hand' (or positive) version is fundamentally different from its 'left-hand' (or negative) version. And a recognition that the right-hand version and the left-hand version cannot be turned in such a way that they become interchangeable, or identical, may, I believe help to explain Shakespeare's own 'on the one hand, on the other hand' portrayals of virtues and vices and villains and victims and justice and mercy—and the ways of gods and mortals—in *Measure for Measure*. Through assigning him dubious motives, then through Lucio, Shakespeare gives us a 'left-hand' version of the Duke, even as he gives the most profound of all the moral recognitions in the play ('Most dangerous/Is that temptation that doth goad us on/To sin in loving virtue') to the most sinister of all its characters. Thus, Mistress Overdone, 'a Bawd of eleven years' continuance' has (on the other hand) taken care of Lucio's child for 'a year and a quarter' (III.ii. 184–91). Claudio is sentenced to death for having 'got his friend with child' (I.iv. 29), and Julietta is morally condemned for a 'sin of heavier kind than his' (II.iii. 28), and so their 'most offenceful act' is negatively associated with sin and death; yet their lover's 'embrace', engendering new life itself, is positively associated with health and nature:

> Your brother and his lover have embrac'd,
> As those that feed grow full, as blossoming time
> That from the seedness the bare fallow brings
> To teeming foison, even so her plenteous womb
> Expresseth his full tilth and husbandry.
>
>   (I.iv. 40–4)

And this, the one and only image of sex in *Measure for Measure* that is not associated with blackmail, rape, prostitution, force or trickery or wrong or shame or sin or disease, but is positively beautiful, is given, by Shakespeare, to Lucio. Yet Lucio informs on Mistress Overdone. And so forth, and so on: there is a right-hand version and a left-hand version of everything and everyone in the world of this play, and the positive and negative properties of the same thing (e.g. 'sacred chastity' or sexual desire) cannot be made identical. In *Measure for Measure*, as in Pasteur's theory, one kind of structure links 'all the forms'—and forces—of life. The question left open in the play, as in the theory, is 'Why?'.

Negatively speaking, its left-hand/right-hand properties are the generators of all the sexual, moral and political confusion in the play, as well as the consequent critical confusion about the sexual, moral and political message we ought to derive from the play. Positively speaking, they are the generators of its dramatic energy and power, since they are what emotionally and intellectually engage the audience in an active and enduring conflict between them:

Escalus	What news abroad i' th' world?
Duke	None, but that there is so great a fever on goodness that the dissolution of it must cure it. Novelty is only in request, and, as it is, as dangerous to be aged in any kind of course as it is virtuous to be constant in any undertaking. There is scarce truth enough alive to make societies secure; but security enough to make fellowships accurst. Much upon this riddle runs the wisdom of the world. This news is old enough, yet it is every day's news.

(III.ii. 208–17)

It is as if Shakespeare deliberately looses conventional dramatic and moral moorings to explore a domain of experience where 'prayers cross' (II.ii. 159), where the wisdom of the world runs upon riddles, and where conflicting virtues and values may be comparably positive, comparably negative: the left hand of liberty is lawlessness; the left hand of righteousness is cruelty, and so on. On the one hand, 'This news is old enough'; on the other hand, 'it is every day's news'.

Moreover, as the words of Marco Mincoff both illustrate and describe, Isabella, Claudio and Angelo take us along with them on the way to temptation where 'prayers cross' and so force us to experience their conflicts on a passionate and personal as well as an intellectual level. For Shakespeare initially portrays the conflicts between these characters 'in a language so pregnant and splendid that it lends to them an added significance and an added depth, so that they seem both larger and truer than life'. It gives us a girl, with an ideal of inviolability–chastity–integrity that seems comparable to the fiery asceticism of a medieval saint, who confronts 'the necessity of consigning her own brother to death, turning from him in horror when he sinks to the level of her tempter'. It gives us her brother, 'brought up to regard death as preferable to dishonour and steeling himself to meet it steadfastly, yet breaking down when a hope of life offers itself'. And it gives us 'a man who believes he is more than his fellows, who stumbles and falls, and struggles blindly to understand how he has become the thing he despises'. The true meaning of Angelo, for Mincoff, may lie in the 'fact that we have experienced his fall with him ... have felt his very repressions bursting out with double force, and his bewilderment when the staff he has always relied on, his freedom from temptation, collapses under him' and 'that we have felt, even in him, some of the potential splendour of humanity' (for full discussion, see Mincoff 1966, pp. 141–52).

Thus it is possible for some of us to pity, even as we condemn, Shakespeares's fallen angel, just as we may pity Milton's, because we share his horror and his suffering as he looks within, and back to his lost virtue:

                    Dark'n'd so, yet shown
        Above them all th' Arch-Angel: but his face
        Deep scars of Thunder had intrencht, and care
        Sat on his faded cheek.

                          Cruel his eye, but cast
        Signs of remorse and passion.

                          (*Paradise Lost*, I. 599–602, 604–5)

Moreover, in a play which would seem to suggest that the
Devil sometime should be honoured for his burning throne,
it is Angelo who faces what may well be the 'most
dangerous' of all temptations to confront a human being
(e.g. 'to sin in loving virtue')—and who finally condemns
himself more severely than anyone else on the stage:

        I am sorry that such sorrow I procure;
        And so deep sticks it in my penitent heart
        That I crave death more willingly than mercy;
        'Tis my deserving, and I do entreat it.

                          (V.i. 472–5)

In contrast to Angelo, the Duke who stands at the 'top of
judgment' at the end of *Measure for Measure* displays no
wounds or scars, nor does he blame himself for all the
sorrow *he* procured; nor does he finally take his full measure
of blame for the social, sexual and legal mess he brought in
Angelo to clean up for him. The Duke is an unusual figure of
ultimate authority in Shakespearian drama in that he does
not, finally, arrive at a conclusion, or have to confront a
conclusion, similar to the one on the sign on President
Harry Truman's desk: 'The Buck Stops Here'. 'I have', cries
King Lear, taken 'Too little care of this!', even as Prospero
himself acknowledges that his own neglect of duty

encouraged Antonio to usurp his dukedom. In *Measure for
Measure*, the Duke, who allows no such 'evasion' to Angelo,
consistently 'passes the buck' of responsibility and guilt to
others. But that, along with his arbitrariness, might make
him the most accurate, as well as the most profoundly
ambivalent, of all dramatic images of the Power, 'who Man
of Baser Earth didst make', and 'ev'n with Paradise' devised
'the Snake': 'For all the Sin wherewith the Face of Man/Is
blackened—man's forgiveness give—and take!' (*The
Rubáiyát of Omar Khayyám*, stanza 31).

It seems to me that the behaviour of the Duke raises the
most ancient of unanswerable questions: 'Is there
unrighteousness with God? God forbid.'

> For he saith to Moses, I will have mercy on whom I will
> have mercy, and I will have compasssion on whom I will
> have compassion.
> So that it is not of him that willeth, nor of him that
> runneth, but of God that sheweth mercy.
> For the scripture saith unto Pharaoh. Even for this
> same purpose have I raised thee up, that I might shew my
> power in thee, and that my name might be declared
> throughout all the earth.
> Therefore hath he mercy on whom he will have mercy,
> and whom he will he hardeneth.
> Thou wilt say then unto me, Why doth he yet find
> fault? For who hath resisted his will?
>
> (Romans, 9:15–19)

As A. P. Rossiter has observed, Shakespeare may well feel
'that there would perhaps be more humanity and kindness
in a world of Pompeys and Lucios, than in one of Isabellas
and Dukes of dark corners' (Rossiter 1961, p. 166). But 'we
do not know'. Pompey, 'Servant to Mistress Overdone',
once imprisoned and with the promise of remission
becomes, 'with no sense of betrayal, servant to the State in
no less a capacity than that of hangman' (on these points see

Dollimore 1985, pp. 72ff). For that matter, the original state of things in Vienna is temporally associated with the world's oldest profession, even as it is metaphysically associated with Original Sin, and the sexual licence reigning in the city is never unequivocally portrayed as a *positively* anarchic, carnivalesque freedom from repression and restraint. It is negatively portrayed in terms of a sleazy, commercial 'trade', involving pimps and madams and brothels and informers and pay-offs, and described as if it were a venereal disease infecting the whole of society. And the first question raised in the play is, 'What, if anything, can, or ought, to be done about it?' Claudio himself describes 'too much liberty' as a lethally addictive form of poison:

> Lucio   Why, how now, Claudio, whence comes this
> restraint?
> Claudio   From too much liberty, my Lucio, liberty;
> As surfeit is the father of much fast,
> So every scope by the immoderate use
> Turns to restraint. Our natures do pursue,
> Like rats that ravin down their proper bane,
> A thirsty evil; and when we drink we die.
> Lucio   If I could speak so wisely under arrest,
> I would send for certain of my creditors;
> and yet, to say the truth, I had as lief have
> the foppery of freedom as the morality of
> imprisonment.
>
> (I.ii. 118–27)

Query: who wouldn't prefer an 'upside down world' where 'liberty plucks justice by the nose' to Angelo's alternative? Moreover, as Summers, Donaldson and Rossiter alike remind us, 'the world upside down' is a fairly normal condition in comedy. But as Donaldson also observes, the question 'Who's in charge?' is commonly raised when dramatic worlds turn upside down—or right side up. And given the fact that the Duke is here responsible for both inversions, the last of all the social, sexual, legal and moral questions raised by *Measure for Measure* is: 'What, if anything, has been accomplished by the Duke's various efforts to alter the *general* state of things in Vienna for the better?' It could be (see Edwards 1968, p.116) that the answer to *this* question is 'Nothing'. And it may well have to be: no one yet has 'found out the remedy' for original sin generally or temporally—only individually, spiritually.

'The Properties of Government': Temporal Justice, Christian Mercy and the Rule of Law

'If you are not confused, you do not understand the situation.'

(Graffiti, in Northern Ireland)

Oh wearisome condition of Humanity!
Born under one law, to another bound:
. . . .
Created sick, commanded to be sound:
What meaneth Nature by these diverse laws?
Passion and Reason self-division cause:
Is it the mark or majesty of Power
To make offences that it may forgive?
Nature herself doth her own self deflower,
To hate those errors she herself doth give.

(Fulke Greville, *Chorus Sacerdotum*)

None does offend, none—I say none.

(Shakespeare, *King Lear*)

Merciful Heaven,
Thou rather, with thy sharp and sulphurous bolt,
Splits the unwedgeable and gnarled oak
Than the soft myrtle. But man, proud man,
Dress'd in a little brief authority,

Most ignorant of what he's most assur'd,
His glassy essence, like an angry ape,
Plays such fantastic tricks before high heaven
As makes the angels weep.

(Shakespeare, *Measure for Measure*)

At the end of *Measure for Measure*, the Duke's own decrees are as 'dead to infliction' as they were in the beginning. In the beginning, the Duke described the 'most biting laws' of Vienna with the royal possessive ('*We* have strict statutes' ... '*our* decrees') and appeared to believe that they should not be amended, or stricken from the books, but must now be strictly enforced as a matter of social and moral necessity. They are the 'needful bits and curbs to headstrong steeds', without which 'liberty plucks justice by the nose'. This is the paramount political reason the Duke gives for investing Angelo with his 'terror' (I.i. 20–2; I.iii. 19–43). Yet the Duke also insists that only a judge who is, himself, blameless, should unleash the law on others:

He who the sword of heaven would bear
Should be as holy as severe;
. . . .
More nor less to others paying,
Than by self-offences weighing.
Shame to him whose cruel striking
Kills for faults of his own liking!

(III.ii. 243–50)

The moral assumption here is unexceptionable. But where does it leave (a) the rule of law itself and (b) the defendant in a criminal trial? The Duke subsequently argues that it would be 'just' for Angelo to condemn Claudio to death for the most venial of all the sexual offences in the play; that is, so long as Angelo

> doth with holy abstinence subdue
> That in himself which he spurs on his pow'r
> To qualify in others. Were he meal'd with that
> Which he corrects, then were he tyrannous;
> But this being so, he's just.
>
> (IV.ii. 77–81)

Neither the severity of Claudio's sentence, nor the severity of the statute itself, is challenged by the Duke: the virtue of the judge is what is on trial.

> *Duke*   If [Angelo's] own life answer the straitness of his
> proceeding, it shall become him well: wherein if
> he chance to fail, he hath sentenc'd himself.
>
> (III.ii. 238–40)

Thus, given the Duke's line of reasoning here, the same defendant (i.e. Claudio) would be (a) justly sentenced to death or (b) unjustly condemned to death under the same statute against illicit sexual intercourse entirely depending on whether (a) he had been sentenced by a holy and abstemious judge or (b) had been sentenced by a lascivious judge, whose verdict should be qualified according to his own sexual culpabilities and proclivities (see Eagleton 1986, p. 56). Therefore, if Angelo had proved to be as 'holy' as he was 'severe', then Claudio (according to the Duke) would have been *justly* sentenced to death under Vienna's 'most biting' of laws (see Bawcutt 1984, p. 91).

Here, as elsewhere in *Measure for Measure*, the applicability of Christ's moral dicta to temporal justice (and mercy) is two-pronged, and itself seems contradictory: 'Judge not, that ye be not judged ... With what measure ye mete, it shall be measured to you again.' As you judge others, so you will be judged; therefore you had better not judge anyone severely, if at all. For how can you know that,

so placed, you might not have so offended? Moreover, even
if you are currently blameless on one count, you cannot be
sure that you always will be—or that you might not be
comparably culpable on another count (say a lack of
charity). The question is whether these Christian precepts
are applicable to magistrates. If so, they amount to a
commandment to command them from their function: it is
their business to judge. And, arguably anyway, to have
'nothing but *mercy, mercy*', and so have 'the extremity of the
law executed on no man' is 'the high way to abolish laws'
and 'in the end to open a door to all confusion, disorder, and
to all licentiousness of life'.

On the other hand, the Scriptures also imply (even as the
Duke does) that it is all right to be as severe to others as you,
yourself, are holy. Angelo would thus be entitled to 'cast
out the mote' in Claudio's eye so long as there is no beam in
his own. Christ's statement, 'He that is without sin among
you, let him first cast a stone' (at the woman taken in the act
of adultery; see p. 7), can likewise be interpreted in two
different ways. I believe it means that no one should cast the
first stone. After all, Christ did not throw one, even though
He was, presumably, 'without sin'. Yet you can interpret
Christ's ruling (even as the Duke interprets Angelo's
judgement of Claudio) to mean that it would be just to stone
the woman to death, 'as Moses in the law commanded', so
long as the stone-throwers themselves are 'without sin' and
stand acquitted by their own consciences. These, and other,
counter-arguments concerning justice, mercy and the rule of
law are eloquently articulated by the various characters in
Measure for Measure, and—yet again—individual members
of the audience are left to decide which, if any, of them to
concur with or reject. For, as Thomas Hobbes observed,

> though the nature of that we conceive, be the same; yet
> the diversity of our reception of it, in respect of different
> constitutions of body, and prejudices of opinion, gives
> everything a tincture of our different passions. ... For one

> man calleth ... *cruelty*, what another *justice*; one
> *prodigality*, what another *magnanimity*. ... From the same
> it proceedeth, that men give different names, to one and
> the same thing, from the difference of their own passions.
>
> (Hobbes 1968, pp. 109, 165)

If this holds true off-stage (e.g. in critical arguments about
the characters and conflicts in *Measure for Measure*) it also
holds true of the differing arguments posited about, and
altogether different descriptions of, the 'same thing' (e.g.
'justice') by the various characters on stage.

In her various arguments in favour of mercy, Isabella
never questions the *justice* of the verdict whereby Claudio
was 'Condemn'd upon the act of fornication/To lose his
head' (V.i. 69–71):

> There is a vice that most I do abhor,
> And most desire should meet the blow of justice.
>
> (II.ii. 29–30)

> O just but severe law.
>
> (II.ii. 41)

She nevertheless appeals to 'custom and practice':

> O, let him marry her!
>
> (I.iv. 49)

> Who is it that hath died for this offence?
> There's many have committed it.
>
> (II.ii. 88–9)

And (like Escalus, II.i. 8–16, and the Duke) she also insists
that the judge should weigh his own conscience in the
balance with the guilt of the defendant:

> Go to your bosom,
> Knock there, and ask your heart what it doth know
> That's like my brother's fault. If it confess
> A natural guiltiness such as is his,
> Let it not sound a thought upon your tongue
> Against my brother's life.
>
> (II.ii. 136–41)

In addition to these specifics, Isabella most eloqently appeals to Christian mercy on the highest of temporal levels—

> No ceremony that to great ones longs,
> Not the king's crown nor the deputed sword,
> The marshal's truncheon nor the judge's robe,
> Become them with one half so good a grace
> As mercy does.
>
> (II.ii. 59–63)

—as well as on the highest of all spiritual levels:

> Why, all the souls that were were forfeit once;
> And He that might the vantage best have took
> Found out the remedy.
>
> (II.ii. 73–5)

Later on, of course, Isabella argues that Angelo should not be *legally* judged according to his natural guiltiness (as, in intent, 'a murderer', and a 'virgin-violator': V.i. 39–41):

> I partly think
> A due sincerity govern'd his deeds
> Till he did look on me; since it is so,
> Let him not die. My brother had but justice,
> In that he did the thing for which he died;
> For Angelo,
> His act did not o'ertake his bad intent,

> And must be buried but as an intent
> That perish'd by the way. Thoughts are no subjects;
> Intents but merely thoughts.
>
> (V.i. 443–52)

Throughout *Measure for Measure*, Isabella argues on a shifting, contextual, basis (see Eagleton 1967, pp. 74–5). What is a cardinal sin in one set of circumstances (her own) is a laudable act in another set of circumstances (Mariana's). Angelo's 'natural guiltiness' is deemed of no importance in her legal case for his defence; but it was of the utmost importance in her moral case for the defence of Claudio. On the one hand, we must look in our hearts before we condemn our brothers (II.ii 136–41); on the other hand, 'We cannot weigh our brother with ourself':

> Great men may jest with saints: 'tis wit in them;
> But in the less foul profanation.
>
> (II.ii.127–8)

Does Isabella here concur with Blake: 'One Law for the Lion & Ox is oppression'? Does her distinction between 'Great men' and 'the less' reflect a spiritual distinction or a social *reality*? Very like a lawyer defending a young offender 'with a good family background', Escalus pleads for the mitigation of Claudio's sentence on social and familial grounds: 'this gentleman … had a most noble father' (II.i. 6–7). And there is no doubt that, today as yesterday, the situational (social, financial, political, sexual) status of the defendant may have as much to do with the verdict rendered, as the personal prejudices or passions of the judge or jury. For that matter, throughout *Measure for Measure*, as in *King Lear*, there is a profoundly nihilistic view of *all* earthly judgements, all justice, all authority—

> Because authority, though it err like others,
> Hath yet a kind of medicine in itself
> That skins the vice o'th'top.
>
> (II.ii. 134–5)

Compare *King Lear* IV.vi. 159–67:

> There thou mightst behold the great image of
>   authority: a dog's obey'd in office.
> Thou rascal beadle, hold thy bloody hand.
> Why dost thou lash that whore? Strip thy own back;
> Thou hotly lusts to use her in that kind
> For which thou whip'st her. The userer hangs the
>   cozener.
> Through tattered clothes small vices doth appear;
> Robes and furr'd gowns hide all. Plate sin with gold,
> And the strong lance of justice hurtless breaks;
> Arm it in rags, a pigmy's straw does pierce it.

Moreover, as Hobbes observed, there is no such thing as an *unprejudiced* judgement on the part of an individual inevitably swayed by his or her own personal situation and familial affections, or by social or sexual or ideological or religious prejudices and convictions. All of us are comparable to Isabella and the Duke, in that our judgements, including our judgements of the characters in *Measure for Measure*, are likewise *ad hoc*, contextual, personal or situational. Or so the dialectically opposite verdicts arrived at by differing critics concerning Isabella, the Duke, Angelo, Claudio, Lucio *et al.*, as well as the generally lenient verdict on the drunken murderer, Barnardine (practically everyone *likes him*), would seem to demonstrate.

Yet it is also true in life, as in Shakespearian drama generally, that most people agree that it is egregiously *unjust*, in the cases of different people manifestly guilty of the identical crime, when one—say the 'Great' man, or the one we most abhor—gets off scot-free, while, say, 'the less'—or the ones we, personally, like, or are related to—are severely punished. This is why Angelo insists that all offenders should be sentenced, alike, according to the law: 'Were [Claudio] my kinsman, brother, or my son,/It should be

thus with him'. Yet most of us would also agree that
extenuating circumstances should be taken into account.
The open questions are 'Which ones?' and 'Whose—if not
all'?: Claudio's? Angelo's? Barnardine's? Ours? Those of
'Humanity/Born under one law, to another bound'? '[H]e's
guilty and he is not guilty', says Diana of Bertram in *All's
Well That Ends Well* (V.iii. 283). Query: who isn't?

Looked back at from a moral angle, Isabella's pleas for
mercy, taken together, likewise tend towards a universal
condemnation (all are guilty in one way or another) that
results, paradoxically, in a universal acquittal: given original
sin, all the souls that ever were were forfeit once, and we'd
all fare badly if 'He, which is at the top of judgement',
should but judge us as we are. We therefore should examine
our own heart's intent, and if it confess a 'natural guiltiness',
it should not 'sound a thought' against another's life. On the
other hand, our worst intentions, desires and criminal
susceptibilities cannot, and should not, be *legally* judged in
the same way as the most venial of our illegal acts.

There are obvious reasons to delight in the moral,
intellectual and structural dialectic whereby, in the end of
the play, Angelo—a character guilty of grievous criminal
intent—is legally exonerated, and Claudio—a character
who was guilty-as-charged under the law, since he did, of his
own free will, commit the act for which he was condemned
to death but was innocent of any evil intent (wilfully,
feloniously and with malice aforethought to blackmail, to
rape, to kill)—are pardoned along with Barnardine, who
actually committed murder, but presumably without malice
aforethought, and while under the influence of alcohol.
Thus Shakespeare suggests that, given universal guilt of one
kind or another, ultimate mercy and grace must be granted
to any one, or to all, of us *independently* of moral
exoneration *or* our just deserts. And so he dramatically
encourages us to grant mercy even unto the *least* deserving
of all characters portrayed on the stage—even unto our
worst enemy, to the character we, personally, most abhor,

and most desire should meet the blow of justice.

Looked at in terms of temporal authority, however, the Duke's mercy seems strained in a way that Shakespeare's compassion for his characters is not. For instance, the Duke's rhetoric verbally (i.e. dramatically) implies that his 'pardon' is granted to Claudio, not because the severity of the sentence was all out of proportion to Claudio's act (or intent), but for Isabella's 'lovely sake'. There are valid moral reasons why Claudio should be pardoned; but the reason the Duke gives is not a moral one. Or is it? After all, a god may pardon a sinner on account of the intercession of a saint. And the Duke himself urges Isabella to pardon Angelo, 'for Mariana's sake' (I.v. 401). But so far as temporal justice is concerned, should the verdict finally rendered in a criminal case be influenced by the judge's (e.g., the Duke's) personal admiration, or affection, for the defendant's lovely sister, any more than it should be determined by the judge's (e.g., Angelo's) lust for her?

> *Isabella* My brother did love Juliet,
>   And you tell me that he shall die for't.
> *Angelo*   He shall not, Isabel, if you give me love
>   (II.iv. 142–4)
>
> *Duke*   If he be like your brother, for his sake
>   Is he pardon'd, and for your lovely sake
>   Give me your hand, and say you will be mine,
>   He is my brother too ...
>   (V.1. 488–91, Folio punctuation)

The Duke's speech is punctuated in differing ways in different editions of *Measure for Measure*. In the Folio, the lack of punctuation at the end of line 489 and the 'and' in the middle of it creates the ambiguity, but it sounds as if the Duke is pardoning Claudio as much for Isabella's 'lovely sake' as for any other reason.

Obviously the Duke's intentions towards Isabella are

honourable, as Angelo's were not; but one still wonders (as Captain Vere puts it in Melville's *Billy Budd*) whether an 'upright judge' ought to allow his verdict in a criminal trial to be determined by his feelings for 'some tender kinswoman of the accused'. In any event, it seems to me that the answer to the question, 'Where is the (temporal) justice in the Duke's treatment of Claudio?'—both when he gives him *no* hope of a pardon in Act 3, and when he grants him an official pardon in Act 5—remains wide open to dispute.

The difficulties of reconciling the claims of justice, divine law (or divine mercy), and the temporal rule of law, that arise throughout *Measure for Measure* have been subjects of literature from Sophocles's *Antigone* on through Melville's *Billy Budd* (see the Appendix below). But they are not (alas) only, or essentially, literary difficulties, problems, conflicts. In our imperfect world, as in *Measure for Measure*, the realm of law is a domain of judgement and choice that conflicts with the realm of Christian idealism where all judgements are ultimately regarded as simple: 'Forgive your enemies'; 'Judge not that ye be not judged'. And it could be that there is no earthly way for Shakespeare, or the Duke, or anyone else to reconcile them any more than there is a way to make the left hand identical to, or interchangeable with, the right hand. This may explain why, in other plays where the justice–mercy conflict arises, Shakespeare often tends to draw clear lines of demarcation between divine mercy, an individual's personal forgiveness, and a governor's duty to enforce the law. King Henry V, for instance, thus distinguishes between God's mercy, his own renunciation of vengeance, and the legal sentence issued:

> God quit you in his mercy! Hear your sentence.
> . . . .
> Touching our person seek we no revenge;
> But we our kingdom's safety must so tender,
> Whose ruin you have sought, that to her laws
> We do deliver you.
> (*Henry V*, II.ii. 166–77)

In marked contrast to the Duke in *Measure for Measure*, Henry readily pardons a drunk who slandered him personally, but he lets the law take its course with the traitors. In Shakespeare's other comedies, as in *The Merchant of Venice*, the law is got round by technicalities, but it is not arbitrarily invoked, and then just as arbitrarily ignored, by the person in authority responsible for law-enforcement. For instance, in *The Merchant of Venice*, the Duke is very sorry for Antonio, and does his best to get Shylock to qualify his rigorous course, but Antonio himself realises that 'The Duke cannot deny the course of law', and Portia concurs:

> there is no power in Venice
> Can alter a decree established;
> 'Twill be recorded for a precedent,
> And many an error, by the same example,
> Will rush into the state.

(IV.i. 213–17)

It would be different if Duke Vincentio, long absent, had returned to overthrow a cruel tyrant. But here the Duke himself initiates the action of the play by insisting on the necessity for strict law-enforcement (as a direct result of his own previous permissiveness) and then proceeds, in an *ad hoc* way, to make sure that the most strict statutes and most biting laws of Vienna are as dead to infliction by the end of the play as they were in the beginning ('Blessed are they that run around in circles, for they shall become wheels'?). Angelo's determination to enforce the law obviously proved to be an unacceptable alternative. Yet Angelo's various arguments concerning the rule of law have strong support from the Duke's last, as well as his first, conclusions about the need for law-enforcement in Vienna:

Duke   ... My business in this state
              Made me a looker-on here in Vienna,
              Where I have seen corruption boil and bubble
              Till it o'errun the stew: laws for all faults,
              But faults so countenanc'd that the strong
                   statutes
              Stand like the forfeits in a barber's shop,
              As much in mock as mark.

                                   (V.i. 314–20)

Angelo is by no means the only character in *Measure for Measure*, or in Shakespearian drama generally, to insist that 'We must not make a scarecrow of the law' (II.i. 1). Nor is he the only character in Shakespearian drama to uphold the rule of law:

Angelo   It is the law, not I condemn your brother.
             Were he my kinsman, brother, or my son,
             It should be thus with him.

                                    (II.ii. 80–2)

A cluster of Shakespearian associate justices—the Duke in *Othello* (I.iii. 67–70), Henry V, and the Lord Chief Justice of England (2 *Henry IV*, V.ii. 70–117)—would assent to this insistence on an impartial enforcement of the law. Moreover, Angelo's statements about precedence and deterrence have support from Escalus as well as from the Duke himself (compare the Duke's speech in I.iii. 19–29):

Angelo   The law hath not been dead, though it hath
                 slept.
             Those many had not dar'd to do that evil
             If the first that did th'edict infringe
             Had answer'd for his deed. Now 'tis awake
             Takes note of what is done, and, like a prophet,
             Looks in a glass that shows what future evils—
             Either now or by remissness new conceiv'd,

And so in progress to be hatch'd and born—
Are now to have no successive degrees,
But here they live to end.

Isabella   Yet show some pity.
Angelo   I show it most of all when I show justice;
For then I pity those I do not know,
Which a dismiss'd offence would after gall,
And do him right that, answering one foul wrong,
Lives not to act another.

(II.ii. 90–104)

. . . .

Justice   Lord Angelo is severe.
Escalus   It is but needful:
Mercy is not itself that oft looks so;
Pardon is still the nurse of second woe.
But yet, poor Claudio! There is no remedy.

(II.i.268–71)

What seems specially interesting about all this is that, with the noteworthy exception of the pimp, Pompey, *everyone* describes the statutes of Vienna as if, like the law of Moses, they were engraved on tablets of stone from on high. Pompey, by contrast, suggests that a temporal law might, conceivably be adjusted to conform with the biological laws of human nature:

Escalus   How would you live, Pompey—by being a bawd? What do you think of the trade, Pompey? Is it a lawful trade?
Pompey   If the law would allow it, sir.
Escalus   But the law will not allow it, Pompey; nor it shall not be allowed in Vienna.
Pompey   Does your worship mean to geld and splay all the youth of the city?

Escalus   No, Pompey.
Pompey   Truly, sir, in my poor opinion, they will to't
          then.

(II.i. 212–21)

The effects of the Viennese prohibition of illicit sex seem markedly comparable to the effects of the Volstead Act prohibiting the consumption of alcohol in the United States.

Perhaps significantly, however, the word 'needful' is strongly associated with the law, and with law-enforcement, by the Duke ('the needful bits and curbs to headstrong steeds') and by Escalus ('It is but needful. ... Pardon is still the nurse of second woe'). In the first acts of *Measure for Measure* the law would seem to serve as a kind of dramatic metaphor *for* necessity; for a social necessity, a moral necessity, an *absolute* necessity, albeit a tragic necessity, a dire necessity, a blind necessity. Even Angelo would 'not deny' the sheer arbitrariness, or the inequity, or the injustice, involved in the way the law may be enforced:

> I not deny
> The jury, passing on the prisoner's life,
> May in the sworn twelve have a thief or two
> Guiltier than him they try. What's open made to
>   justice,
> That justice seizes. What knows the laws
> That thieves do pass on thieves?

(II.i. 18–23)

Thus Claudio's statement about the 'demigod Authority' has obvious applicability to law-enforcement in general. Like a law prohibiting fornication, the law, 'Thou shalt not steal', may make us 'pay down for our offence by weight/The words of heaven': on whom it will, it will; on whom it will not, so: 'yet still 'tis just' (I.ii. 114–17). Regardless of the fact that 'thieves do pass on thieves', the

law against theft itself is 'just' *in so far as* 'the moral
imperative behind the law remains constant' (Ornstein
1960, p. 253).

In other Shakespearian comedies, the laws set down on
earth are neither so strongly associated with the laws 'set
down in heaven', nor are the laws of heaven and of earth and
of human nature shown to be so profoundly at odds with
eath other. There is, however, a similar emphasis on the
temporal necessity for law-enforcement, and on the duty of
the governor to uphold the rule of law, however silly or
cruel it may seem to enforce it in individual cases. In *A
Midsummer-Night's Dream*, for instance, Shakespeare
explicitly contrasts the magical domain of Oberon, where
the characters are free from law (and necessity) with the
realm of Theseus, who must rule by the statutes of Athens:

> For you, fair Hermia, look you arm yourself
> To fit your fancies to your father's will [and marry
>   Demetrius]
> Or else the law of Athens yields you up—
> Which by no means we may extenuate—
> To death, or to a vow of single life.

> (I.i. 117–21)

Oberon's intervention is what obviates the necessity for the
law to be enforced by Theseus, since Demetrius finally loves
Helena.

Time after time, in Shakespearian comedy, the action is
devised to liberate the comic heroes and heroines from the
domain of necessity, which is strongly associated with some
law. After all, the domain of necessity is, so far as drama is
concerned, the domain of tragedy. You can, therefore, see
the tragi-comic movement of *Measure for Measure* in this
light: in the first part, the major characters are portrayed as
subject, by law or by their own psychological or biological
nature, to tragic (or potentially tragic) necessities and
consequences. In the second half of the play, necessity is got

round by the Duke, acting as a kind of *deus ex machina* in order to avert tragic consequences, and to emancipate the other characters from dire necessity. Dramatically, as well as socially, the Duke's contrivances and evasions, and final pardons to everyone on the criminal docket, in effect revoke (or transcend) the rule of law, and to revoke (or transcend) the rule of law is to negate necessity. Shakespeare thus incorporates what had originally been portrayed as tragic—or potentially tragic—conundrums, imperatives, and necessities, into a kind of divine comedy. Yet when it is looked at in terms of the original characterisation, this containment, or transformation, in effect deprives various characters of the dignity that comes from confronting the consequences of their own actions, decisions and desires. In the end, Angelo seems to be pleading for that dignity—for necessity, for consequences and, paradoxically, for the freedom to confront them—when he pleads for death. One could argue that, by denying him that dignity, that freedom, the Duke seasons mercy with justice—comic characters who see themselves as tragic characters are often put down at the end of a play. But it can also be argued that, in altering the focus and action of the play from tragic necessities to comic compromises, and evasions of necessity, Shakespeare, by breaching it, may in effect call our attention to an essential decorum described in a tale by Isak Dinesen.

[Tragedy is] a noble phenomenon, the noblest on earth. But of the earth only, and never divine. Tragedy is the privilege of man, his highest privilege. The God of the Christian Church Himself, when He wished to experience tragedy, had to assume human form. And even at that ... the tragedy was not wholly valid, as it would have become had the hero of it been, in very truth, a man. The divinity of Christ conveyed to it a divine note, the moment of comedy. The real tragic part, by the nature of things, fell to the executors, not the victim.... Tragedy should remain the right of human beings, subject, in their conditions or in their own nature, to the dire law of necessity. To them it is salvation and beatification. But the gods, whom we must believe to be unacquainted with and incomprehensive of necessity, can have no knowledge of the tragic. When they are brought face to face with it they will, according to my experience, have the good taste and decorum to sit still, and not interfere.... [And] we, who stand in lieu of the gods and have emancipated ourselves from the tyranny of necessity, should leave to our vassals their monopoly of tragedy.... Only a boorish and cruel master—a parvenu, in fact—will make a jest of his servants' necessity or force the comic upon them.

> (Dinesen 1961, pp. 52–3)

Looked at this light, the problem with the ending of *Measure for Measure* is that the Duke, who stands 'in lieu of the gods', and has emancipated himself 'from the tyranny of necessity', seems, in effect, to 'force the comic' upon Angelo, and so makes 'a jest' of his servant's necessity.

But it is obviously unfair to blame the Duke for forcing the comic upon the other characters. It is Shakespeare, acting in and through the Duke, who alters the course of the action in Act 3 and shifts the focus of the play from tragic psychological and social and biological realities to comic evasions and intrigues. As we have seen, he may have had good reasons for ending the play as mercifully as he does. It's the way he achieves the resolution that causes problems. As we shall see, a kind of internal dichotomy between the psychological brilliance of Shakespeare's original portrayals of the major characters in the first half of the play, and the mechanistic nature of certain structural contrivances (e.g. the introduction of Mariana, the bed-trick, etc.) involved in the second half of the play, may itself explain why Shakespeare's critical jury remains hopelessly split between those who will, and those who will not, applaud the technical resolution of the action. Those who most admire the resolution tend to focus on the play's construction, on its Christian connotations, on the morally satisfying triumph of mercy and pardon over sin and sinners, and on the necessity *for* compromise, as opposed to absolutism. Those who find the domestic resolutions so bland and perfunctory as to seem a let-down to the audience (as well as patronising to the major characters), or so contrived—so forced—as to call the Duke's official solutions to the problems in question, tend to stress the psychological and dramatic inconsistencies between Shakespeare's initial portrayals of the major characters and his subsequent revelations about Angelo's past, Isabella's future, the inconsistencies of the Duke's motives, and so on (see also Muir 1979, pp. 133–4). Thus, the differing ways of interpreting the play's construction which are surveyed in the next chapter have mandated differing responses to the characterisation, even as differing responses to the individual characters tend to mandate altogether different responses to the construction of the play as a whole.

· 3 ·

Construction and Characterisation
Some Counter-Arguments

The form is mechanic, when on any given material we impress a pre-determined form, not necessarily arising out of the properties of the material;—as when to a mass of wet clay we give whatever shape we wish it to retain when hardened. The organic form, on the other hand, is innate; it shapes, as it develops, itself from within, and the fullness of its development is one and the same with the perfection of its outward form. Such as the life is, such is the form. Nature, the prime genial artist, inexhaustible in diverse powers, is equally inexhaustible in forms ... and even such is the appropriate excellence of her chosen poet, of our own Shakespeare.

(Samuel Taylor Coleridge, *Lectures*)

Much of the critical controversy about the ultimate impact of *Measure for Measure* results from the internal dichotomy between differing kinds of construction and character-isation which, in turn, seem to have been mandated by the tragi-comic structure of the play as a whole. To use Kenneth Burke's terms, in the first half of the play, the decisions and desires of the 'agents' (Angelo, Isabella and Claudio) appear to be determining the course of the action, and the 'scene' (the social, sexual, legal mess in Vienna, i.e. the general context in which the action takes place) is graphically portrayed. In the second half, the 'agency' or agencies (the Duke's—or the playwright's—contrivances through which a comic resolution will finally be achieved) are what determine the behaviour of the other characters and so dictate the subsequent course of the action. (For fuller discussion, see Burke's brilliant account [1962, pp. xviiff] of the differing ways in which the drama may emphasise, or show the interaction between, the 'act' [what happens], the 'scene' [the context in which it happens], the 'agents' [the characters], the 'agency' [the means by which the action is accomplished or completed], and the 'purpose' [the motives for the action].) Thus the social crisis in Vienna, the initial characterisation of the antagonists, Isabella, Claudio and Angelo, and the highly-charged verse through which Shakespeare portrays the conflicts between them, are of paramount importance to the dramatic structure as well as the dramatic power of the first half of the play. They are the energy-sources of the action on-stage, and of its impact on the audience, off-stage. When the Duke takes over, 'as boss', in Act 3 Scene 4, the playwright's dramatic focus and energies shift to various intrigues; the language spoken by the major characters suddenly changes from verse to prose; the pace of the action speeds up; and the action itself (like the introduction of Mariana and her old contract with Angelo, and the substitution of Barnardine, then Ragozine, for Claudio) seems structurally contrived in order to effect a comic resolution. Compare, for instance, the differing kinds of language and the differing kinds of responses (to death and to the violation of 'sacred chastity') that Shakespeare gives to Claudio and Isabella immediately before, and after, the Duke re-enters and takes control of the action.

Claudio   ... 'tis too horrible.
          The weariest and most loathed worldly life
          That age, ache, penury and imprisonment,

	Can lay on nature is a paradise
	To what we fear of death.
Isabella	Alas, alas!
Claudio	Sweet sister, let me live.

Can lay on nature is a paradise
To what we fear of death.
Isabella Alas, alas!
Claudio   Sweet sister, let me live.
What sin you do to save a brother's life,
Nature dispenses with the deed so far
That it becomes a virtue.
Isabella   O you beast!
O faithless coward! O dishonest wretch!
Wilt thou be made a man out of my vice?
Is't not a kind of incest to take life
From thine own sister's shame? What should I
    think?
Heaven shield my mother play'd my father fair!
For such a warped slip of wilderness
Ne'er issu'd from his blood. Take my defiance;
Die, perish. Might but my bending down
Reprieve thee from thy fate, it should proceed.
I'll pray a thousand prayers for thy death,
No word to save thee.
Claudio Nay, hear me, Isabel.
Isabella   O fie, fie fie!
Thy sin's not accidental, but a trade.
Mercy to thee would prove itself a bawd;
'Tis best that thou diest quickly.
Claudio   O, hear me, Isabella.

               [*Re-enter* Duke]
Duke Vouchsafe a word, young sister, but one word.
Isabella What is your will?
Duke Might you dispense with your leisure, I would by and by have some speech with you; the satisfaction I would require is likewise your own benefit.
Isabella I have no superfluous leisure; my stay must be stolen out of other affairs, but I will attend you awhile.   [*walks apart*]

Duke	[To Claudio] Son, I have overheard what hath pass'd between you and your sister. Angelo had never the purpose to corrupt her—only he hath made an assay of her virtue to practise his judgment with the disposition of natures. She, having the truth of honour in her, hath made him that gracious denial which he is most glad to receive. I am confessor to Angelo, and I know this to be true; therefore prepare yourself to death. Do not satisfy your resolution with hopes that are fallible; tomorrow you must die; go to your knees and make ready.
Claudio	Let me ask my sister pardon. I am so out of love with life that I will sue to be rid of it.
Duke	Hold you there. Farewell. Provost, a word with you.
	[Re-enter Provost]
Provost	What's your will, father?
Duke	That, now you are come, you will be gone.

(III.i. 129–75)

Rather like the Duke, who summons the Provost only to dismiss him, Shakespeare here seems to have ignited Isabella's fury, and Claudio's will-to-live, as it were *immediately* to extinguish them.

The reason for the abrupt transition from one kind of dramatic language (and from one kind of dramatic action) to another, seems technical, structural. Except for the purposes of holding the audience—like Claudio?—in suspense concerning the outcome of subsequent intrigues, why should the Duke falsely exculpate Angelo and (yet again) insist that Claudio 'must' die tomorrow? What other purpose is achieved by leaving poor Claudio so 'out of love with life' that he will 'sue to be rid of it'? Subsequently, we have a network of analogous actions, of *quos* for *quids* (see Nuttall 1968), that are brilliantly contrived to avert tragic consequences, vengeance and death. Mariana substitutes her maidenhead for Isabella's, even as the head of the already-dead Ragozine is substituted for the head of Barnardine that was going to substitute for the head of Claudio (see Kott 1978, on 'Heads' and 'Maidenheads'). Angelo is (justly) tricked into committing the same act of fornication for which he had sentenced Claudio to death, even as he is (mercifully) tricked out of committing rape or murder. In the end, various characters ask for and receive pardon: Isabella pardons Angelo for Mariana's sake, and so on. In Act 3 Claudio had pleaded to 'ask [his] sister's pardon' (see above), and in Act 5 Isabella pleads for, and gets, 'pardon' from the Duke for having 'employ'd and pain'd' his 'unknown sovereignty' (V.i. 383–5). The Duke himself does not ask Claudio's pardon for having twice left him with no hope *of* pardon, nor does he ask pardon of Isabella for having falsely informed her that Claudio was dead—presumably because he did so for their moral betterment, but he does grant legal forms of pardon to all the criminal offenders.

It seems to me that the first half of the play (wherein the dramatic form seems to shape, 'as it develops, itself from within') fits Coleridge's definition of 'organic form', even as the decisions and desires of the characters themselves seem to be shaping the course of the action towards a tragic catastrophe: Angelo is absolute for the letter of the law, then absolutely determined to have Isabella; Claudio is absolute for life; Isabella is absolute for chastity. By contrast, the form of the second half of the play seems mechanically (albeit brilliantly) impressed upon the play in order to achieve a comic resolution not 'necessarily arising out of the properties of the material', in so far as the compromises between absolutes (justice, mercy, chastity, etc.) seem imposed upon Shakespeare's raw material. Which kind of action you, personally, prefer, may well depend on whether you prefer the processes of the drama to be concealed or displayed (see below). But in either event it is difficult to deny that there *are* any significant differences between the construction and characterisation in the two halves of the play (see Tillyard 1950, pp. 123–38, for a good discussion of the differences).

Since the artistic, as well as the critical, tradition provides us with alternative ways of thinking about Shakespeare's construction, it is worth citing some generalisations by major playwrights that have obvious relevance to the differing modes of construction and characterisation operative in *Measure for Measure*. Playwrights and poets generally tend to admire Shakespeare's 'organic form' more than the most brilliant of structural mechanisms as it were so rare, so mysterious, so miraculous, as to seem practically inimitable. (*Query*: is the creation of the illusion of organic form itself the most brilliant of all structural mechanisms?) 'What could be easier', asked Dryden (in his *Essay of Dramatic Poesy*) 'than to write a regular play like those of the French?' By contrast, nothing could be more difficult than to write an 'irregular' play, like one by Shakespeare: 'Shakespeare's Magick could not copy'd be,/Within that Circle none durst walk but he' (see Dryden's Prologue to *The Tempest, or The Enchanted Island*). To Shakespeare's earliest admirers, like Dryden, the greatest works of the 'man who of all Modern, and perhaps Ancient Poets, had the largest and most comprehensive soul' seemed more like products of nature than products of conscious artistry, just as they did to Coleridge. And, to some of Shakespeare's twentieth-century admirers, they still do. 'Shakespeare', Bertolt Brecht concluded, 'doesn't need construction'. 'With him everything develops naturally.' His plays are the 'unvarnished representations' of human experience by 'a great realist' without any interest in lending 'arguments not drawn from life' to some 'principle that can only be prejudice'. 'He is naturally unclear.' 'He is absolute matter.'

I have quoted Brecht's conclusions about Shakespeare's construction because—like Dryden's and Coleridge's— they are historically representative as well as demonstrably accurate. After all, as Maurice Morgann (among others) has observed, in drama 'the impression is the fact' and—historically speaking—the main impression conveyed by Shakespeare's construction is that, at its best, it is not *too* good; that is, not too good to be true to life. Therefore, like some of his greatest characters, some of his greatest plays have defied all critical efforts to pluck out the heart of the mystery, to smooth out their elevations and depressions, or to moralise them in ways that will shape, to tidy ends, what Brecht called the 'lot of raw materials' that Shakespeare 'shovels onto the stage'. Thus, throughout the seventeenth and earlier eighteenth century, Shakespeare's construction regularly turned up on the debit side of the *critical* ledger.

To many of Shakespeare's seventeenth- and eighteenth-century admirers, he triumphed in spite of the fact that he violated virtually every known rule of dramatic construction. In his *Preface to Shakespeare*, Dr Johnson gives us a comprehensive list of the structural and moral rules of neoclassical criticism that Shakespeare does not obey. Shakespeare does not, for instance, present us with an intrigue 'regularly perplexed and regularly unravelled'; he does not endeavour 'to hide his design only to discover it'. His plots are often so 'loosely formed' that 'a very slight consideration may improve them'. When he found himself near the end of certain works, he 'shortened the labour to snatch the profit': 'He therefore remits his efforts when he should most vigorously exert them, and his catastrophe is improbably produced or imperfectly represented'. Morally speaking, he makes no 'just distribution of good or evil'. Indeed, he seems to write without 'any moral purpose', and leaves the 'examples' of his virtuous and vicious characters to operate 'by chance' (see Nichol Smith 1916, p.88). Yet transcending any technical liabilities were the supreme assets: the high invention that allows the mind to contemplate well-nigh every possibility, the 'just representations of general nature', and above all, those characters who, beyond any others, have the properties of being believed in and remembered for a lifetime; of seeming unique individuals, yet representatives of a whole 'species' of humankind as well.

Like Brecht, Shakespeare's earliest critics point straight to the most obvious, yet surely the oddest thing about Shakespeare's construction. And that is the fact that, in many of his greatest scenes and plays, you do not notice it. While watching or reading *Measure for Measure*, I still don't notice, or come close to comprehending, the structural components active in the great confrontations between Isabella, Claudio and Angelo. These characters seem to have conscious and subconscious desires all their own. For instance, whether you interpret Claudio's unforgettable response to Isabella's claim that she would willingly throw down her life (as opposed to subjecting her body to most abhorred pollution) for his sake—'Thanks, dear Isabel' (III.i. 107)—as an appropriately ironical put-down or as absolutely sincere, it seems *Claudio's* response. Likewise, Isabella's fiery lines about stripping herself to death as to a bed that 'longing had been sick for' seem her own, not just lines given to her by the playwright for the purposes of furthering the plot. As A. D. Nuttall has observed, in certain instances the greatest poetry in *Measure for Measure* seems to be working, even as the characters themselves appear to be speaking, in ways at odds with the official design, or meaning, of the play. Thus the poetry Shakespeare gives to Isabella—

The sense of death is most in apprehension;
And the poor beetle that we tread upon
In corporal sufferance finds a pang as great
As when a giant dies.

(III.i. 79–82)

—'works as hard for Claudio as it does for her'. 'Let the historicist have his say; "Taken in their context the lines clearly mean that even a giant feels at death no more pain than a beetle does." Of course. But is it pure accident that the common reader has always taken it to mean just the opposite?' (Nuttall 1968, p. 248). I never have been able to figure out whether Angelo's complaint about the tedium of the scene between Elbow, Froth and Pompey—

> This will last out a night in Russia,
> When nights are longest there.
>
> (II.i. 128–9)

—functions to distract our attention from the laboured puns on the names of Elbow ('he's out at elbow', 'I do lean upon justice, sir') and Froth ('[tapsters] will draw you, Master Froth'), or whether it made me realise that the scene was boring me along with Angelo and Escalus (II.i. 111). The scene is structurally crucial: it shows the confusion between benefactors and malefactors; shows Angelo himself leaving Escalus to clean up the mess; hints at Angelo's sadistic hope to see everyone whipped, etc.; but the account of what was done to Elbow's wife does get tiresome (in comparison to, say, the Dogberry scenes in *Much Ado About Nothing*). To have a character on stage complain of being bored is one way to make boredom seem funny; but it could also give voice to the playwright's recognition that the jokes are not up to par. In any event, a scene can be structurally defensible, yet dull, even as lines that serve no apparent structural purpose— and may even seem at odds with the overall construction— may blaze with light.

It should be noted here that the humour in *Measure for Measure* is yet another subject of unending controversy. For instance, the scene just described as comparatively dull has been ably defended by R. A. Foakes as especially lively and very funny (Foakes 1971, pp. 18–19). By somewhat the same token, Dr Johnson found the 'light or comic' parts of this play 'very natural and pleasing'. Conversely, to Coleridge, 'the comic and tragic parts equally border on the μισητόν [hateful], the one disgusting, the other horrible'. For

Dowden, 'the humourous scenes would be altogether repulsive were it not that they are needed to present ... the world of moral licence and corruption out of and above which rise the virginal strength and severity and beauty of Isabella'. Bradley, in turn, found 'humour, of course, but little mirth' in *Measure for Measure* (see Eccles 1980, pp. 395–99). And whereas Lisa Jardine concludes that the 'entire play is rich with sexual banter, bawdy, and open enjoyment of exuberant sexuality' (Jardine 1983, p. 190), Marilyn French concludes that 'although the bawds and Elbow are comic, their dialogue is far from lighthearted' (French 1982, p. 187). To Louise Schleiner the 'humour in *Measure for Measure*' is, on the one hand, 'very funny', but it is, on the other hand, 'a kind of black humour, reinforcing the themes of hollow justice and tyrannous authority' (Schleiner 1982, p. 231). I personally and particularly relish the anti-authoritarian one-liners from Pompey, Barnardine and Lucio; for example:

Duke	You were not bid to speak.
Lucio	No, my good lord;
	Nor wish'd to hold my peace.

(V.i. 78–79)

But *whatever* is alleged to be especially funny or tragic or tragi-comic about this particular play, tends, as often as not, to depend on the critical or directorial interpretation of it being posited—not vice versa. Structurally speaking, the argument 'This is supposed to be funny' can be used to defend whatever scene, or to put down whatever character, you wish to defend or put down.

Arguably anyway, the best scenes and speeches in *Measure for Measure* have a dramatic impact that transcends their structural function, even as they seem to develop so naturally from the characterisation that you do not notice their structural function. So far as creating the illusion of organic form is concerned, it took me years to notice how economically Shakespeare recycles the identical materials so that, say, the gulling of Malvolio and the enlightenment of Benedick are effected by the same trick whereby Character X is persuaded that Character Y is in love with him; and it only recently dawned on me that Claudio, in *Measure for Measure*, is blood-brother to Costard, who 'contrary to established proclaimed edict and continent canon' was, likewise, taken 'with a wench', and that the laws against lovers in both plays elicit a remarkably comprehensive range of responses to the fact that it 'is the simplicity of man to hearken after the flesh' (*Love's Labour's Lost*, I.i. 211, 244–8).

Thus there are good reasons why Maurice Morgann compared Shakespeare to a magician whose art is 'most telling and admirable when it is most concealed'. 'We discern not his course', wrote Morgann, 'We are rapt in ignorant admiration and claim no kindred with his abilities.' 'Whilst we feel and are sensible that the whole is design', all the incidents, all the parts 'look like chance'. 'He commands every passage to our heads and to our hearts, and moulds us as he pleases, and that with so much ease that he never betrays his own exertions.' Consequently, 'it is that art in Shakespeare, which, being withdrawn from our notice, we more emphatically call Nature'. When Shakespeare's construction calls attention to itself, Morgann finds it wanting: 'the over-strict adherence to the Laws of Place and Time, by which he has almost strangled [*The Tempest*] discovers either a Childish Ambition or a peasant-like Acquiescence in the Dictas [*sic*] of some pedantic school' (Morgann 1972, pp. 170–1; see also p. 291). Following these leads, one could argue, with reference to *Measure for Measure*, that it is in those confrontation scenes, when he does *not* betray his own exertions as he does in the course of bringing about the comic resolution via Mariana, Ragozine ("'tis an accident that heaven provides!'), etc., that Shakespeare seems most Shakespearian.

Looked at from another angle, a conscious concern with

the comic and tragic processes of the drama can also be seen as characteristically Shakespearian. It dramatically manifests itself from the beginning of his career (in, say, *Love's Labour's Lost* and *A Midsummer-Night's Dream*) on through *Hamlet* and *The Tempest*. Indeed, it is hard to think of a play by Shakespeare that *cannot* be interpreted in metadramatic terms, or as fundamentally concerned with the nature of the drama itself (see Calderwood 1971, and Righter 1962). For that matter, the most important breakthrough in twentieth-century criticism of Shakespearian drama has surely been the revolutionary change in assumptions concerning Shakespeare's craftsmanship. In a ground-breaking essay on 'Construction in Shakespeare' published in 1951, Hereward Price complained that the best critics and scholars then spent all their time discussing Shakespeare's characterisation without paying any attention to the construction of his plays. And I still remember how Price's brilliant account of the analogous relationships between speech and speech, scene and scene, part and whole, in Shakespeare's earliest works struck those who read it with the force of revelation. Moreover, there is no question that some of the best twentieth-century discussions of Shakespeare have to do with the ways in which he developed modes of construction that originated in medieval drama. As more and more critics jumped on these bandwagons, however, the principles of dramatic counterpoint and thematic unity, of likeness with difference, of analogous action and iterative imagery, came to be treated, in certain scholarly circles, as if they were ends in themselves, as criteria of dramatic merit, in spite of the obvious fact that they may occur in the worst of Elizabethan plays as well as the best. For a time it appeared as if the situation deplored by Hereward Price had been all too effectively reversed, as everything in the plays was accounted for in terms of their thematic unity, or patterns of imagery, or their 'morality-play' structures, while discussions of the characterisation—on which the theatrical survival of the plays had, historically, depended—was deemed so outmoded as to be treated as a critical taboo ('novelty' may be 'only in request' as often in criticism as it is in art or in life). As William Empson observed, there was, obviously, 'a kind of truth' in the recognition that Shakespeare's characters are not amenable to the kind of biographical and psychological scrutiny one might give people in real life; yet the new emphasis on structure and imagery was 'dangerously liable to make us miss points of character' (see Empson 1961, p.69). After all, as the books of John Bayley have eloquently reminded us, it is *through* characters who appear to be acting independently of him that Shakespeare constructed some of his greatest plays.

In her book about *Shakespeare and the Story* (1978), Joan Rees gives us an excellent account of the dialectical dichotomy between various critical conclusions concerning Shakespeare's construction and characterisation which manifests itself in various critical arguments about *Measure for Measure* in particular. In opposition to seventeenth- and eighteenth-century commentators, 'who conspicuously failed to recognise Shakespeare's consummate artistry', much criticism nowadays is characterised by an 'unwillingness to admit that the artistry ever fails' (p.140). Whereas Dr Johnson had found the conclusions of certain plays improbably produced or imperfectly represented, and the action 'so carelessly pursued that [Shakespeare] seems not always to comprehend his own design', Hereward Price concluded that 'Shakespeare's work is a strict intellectual construction developed from point to point until he brings us to the necessary and inevitable conclusion' (see Rees 1978, pp.2–3). Rightly acknowledging that Price's appreciative response to Shakespeare's construction had proved immensely fruitful, Rees points out that his assumptions have also led to numerous discussions that deaden the plays: 'by over-intellectualising and schematising [Shakespeare's] work they misrepresent the leaping life that is in it' (p.4). Pausing to look at the stories as they are being turned into drama, Rees observes that Shakespeare's creative energies sometimes manifest themselves in ways that are destructive of any 'point by point' development of a strict intellectual construction (p. 4). In *Measure for Measure*, there is an 'infusion of creative vigour into the original characterization' which is 'in excess of the scope' provided by the overall framework of the plot (p. 38). One can 'only admire the wonderful manipulative and inventive facility' displayed in Shakespeare's technical solutions to these, and other, problems. Yet there is no denying that in his efforts to avoid leaving a play 'with just one or two brilliant figures, and desolation all around them' (p. 71), Shakespeare sometimes sacrifices character to structure and betrays his own exertions in conclusions that seem improbably produced or imperfectly represented.

Therefore, given differing lines of reasoning and emphasis, and depending on whether they look at the characterisation in terms of the construction (or vice versa) modern critics may interpret the structure of *Measure for Measure* in (at least) five different ways, all of which can be supported by chapter-and-verse quotations from the text. Critic A can argue that the ending of *Measure for Measure* is technically and generically satisfying, given the overt tragi-comic form of the play. Critic B can moralise the ending in terms of the thematic reconciliations of justice and mercy (let Angelo 'marry a good woman and be happy', pleads Leavis 1952, p. 172). Conversely, Critic C can (still) argue that dramatic construction is, after all, only a means to an end, and the end has to justify the means; that in the best scenes in *Measure for Measure* it does just that by *virtue* of the fact that the characters themselves appear to be making up the lines and deciding what they are going to do next; and that when the playwright himself appears to be making up the construction as he goes along, and arbitrarily adapting the characterisation in accordance with it, as he does in the second half of *Measure for Measure* or in, say, the last scenes of *The Two Gentlemen of Verona*, his resolutions seem improbably produced and/or imperfectly represented. Or, as Joan Rees has observed, you can admire and extol the structural ingenuities and the ducal contrivances of the second part of the play, yet still argue that the ending seems comparatively bland and deceptive, since 'the statement of the problems and their resolutions at the end does not match the situations as they were at the beginning' (pp. 70–1). Alternatively, you could acclaim the author for devising a drama that defies all attempts to confine it, including its own ending, in so far as the conflicting arguments, differing visions and differing styles, and even the silences interacting in this strange tragi-comedy, would sometimes seem to confound, as they elsewhere would seem to create, the most perfectly ordered of structures for the thoughts and the actions portrayed. Here, for instance, are some of the brilliant dramatic effects Ann Pasternak Slater has observed as the wheels of the action come full circle at the end of the play:

> The last act opens with Isabella throwing herself at the Duke's feet, calling for the four-times repeated ideal, Justice. Her plea, and her action, are then repeated by Mariana later in the scene, as she too begs for justice in the adjudication of her claims on Angelo. But as soon as Angelo's guilt is clear, and the Duke has pronounced rigid *justice*: 'An Angelo for Claudio, death for death', the pattern is repeated in reverse. Mariana now throws herself down before the Duke, pleading for *mercy* with all the anguish of love.... Mercy is prompted, above all, by love. But it must also be supported by moral logic: Mariana's pleas must be seconded by Isabella, Angelo's victim.
>
> (Pasternak Slater 1982, pp. 74–5)

As Slater also observes, it is 'an indication of *Measure for Measure*'s dialectical neatness that Isabella and Angelo must

both abide by the same painful consistency during its
course':

> Angelo must condemn himself to the death he first meted
> out to Claudio, since their crimes are the same, and it is to
> his credit that he does so sincerely.... And the mercy
> Isabella required for Claudio, she must now beg for
> Angelo.... 'Let him not die: my Brother had but
> Iustice,/In that he did the thing for which he dide./For
> Angelo, His Act did not ore-take/His bad intent....' But
> her argument is more generous than truthful. Angelo may
> not have slept with her, but he did spend the night with
> Mariana, with whom he had a pre-contract (just as
> Claudio had with Juliet). And, as far as Isabella knows, he
> did moreover break his word and kill Claudio—a fact she
> magnanimously glosses over in her plea that the Duke
> should look on Angelo 'As if my Brother liu'd'.

Then, as she begs mercy for Angelo, Claudio seems to rise
from the dead, and Angelo, effectively guiltless by his
resurrection, can live also—they are both like men 'new
made'.

There is no denying the force of these structural
arguments: looked at from one angle, *Measure for Measure* is
one of the most brilliantly constructed plays ever written.
Looked at from another angle, however, the ending seems
unconvincingly represented. Isabella's kneeling alongside
Mariana can appear as puppet-like as her assent to the bed-
trick. She has been as putty in the hands of the Duke ever
since he took charge of the action, so there is no real surprise
when she continues to act as he has planned she should; no
question that she will pass the test he set for her, and plead
for mercy for her enemy. (I am indebted to Dame Helen
Gardner for this argument.) By the same token, the Duke's
god-games designed to 'make her heavenly conforts of
despair, when it is least expected' seem (to some of us) to be

so patronising as to be more infuriating, in intent, than satisfying when dramatically realised. And Mariana is too shadowy a character for her supine love for Angelo (which seems to exist only to solve otherwise insoluble structural problems) to sway an audience emotionally. Looked at from yet another perspective, one could argue that what would seem to be the structural flaws in the ending are the most interesting things about it, since, whether Shakespeare intended them to or not, the contradictions in Isabella's arguments, like those lines about the 'due sincerity' that governed Angelo's deeds before he looked on her, the recalcitrance of Lucio, and the silence of Angelo concerning Mariana, seem, in *effect*, dramatically to reinforce the sense of unresolved problems, of questions left open, that may account for this play's unending fascination and impact.

There is, surely some truth to Maurice Morgann's observation that in drama, the impression is the fact. What is especially odd about *Measure for Measure* is that in spite of the structurally schematic sequence of substitutions, tests and pardons, the play still gives the impression that Shakespeare, like the Duke, was deciding what to do next on the spur of the moment, on an *ad hoc* basis, and did not look back or worry about inconsistencies. This would suggest that the best way to stage *Measure for Measure* is in terms of 'scenic' form; not for consistency of characterisation. If you retrospectively play Angelo as a blatant hypocrite, and so prepare for the revelation about his old contract with Mariana, you lose the dramatic impact of seeing an Angelo, previously invulnerable to temptation, fall. And there seems no way to prepare for the Duke's sudden proposal to Isabella, so let it come as a surprise to the audience. Given even a slight consideration, Shakespeare could have done something to make the Duke's proposal to Isabella seem less inconsistent. But, in the play as it stands, he makes it come as a bolt from the blue (see Barton 1974, p. 548). In Act 1, the Duke emphatically assures Friar Thomas that 'the dribbling dart of love' cannot pierce his 'complete bosom'.

No, holy father; throw away that thought;
Believe not that the dribbling dart of love
Can pierce a complete bosom.

(I.iii. 1–3)

Later on, when Lucio accuses the Duke of being a
womaniser, the Duke-disguised-as-a-friar indignantly insists
that he (himself) 'was not inclin'd that way':

Lucio   [In marked contrast to Angelo, the Duke] had
        some feeling for the sport; he knew the service,
        and that instructed him to mercy.
Duke   I never heard the absent Duke much detected
        for women; he was not inclin'd that way.

(III.ii. 111–14)

And there is *no* subsequent information to the effect that the
dart of love for Isabella has pierced the complete bosom of
the Duke. Why not have the Duke inform the audience that
he regrets being disguised as a friar because he has fallen in
love with Isabella himself? Why not have Isabella reveal a
change in her desire to enter the Convent of St Clare, or
somehow manifest a recognition that the Duke is the man
for her, and that her true vocation is in marriage to him? It
might have seemed simply too lurid to have the Duke, in
disguise as a friar, showing a growing interest in the 'lovely'
self of a novice, or to show that young novice falling in love
with a father-figure in the vestments of a friar. If so, the last-
minute pairing-off of the Duke with Isabella, may,
necessarily, be inconsistent with the original portrayals of
the two characters, albeit structurally necessary to make
everyone leave the stage neatly paired-off with someone else
(see Lever 1965, p. 149). But it takes some critical projection
to argue that Shakespeare's primary effect is to show
Isabella's new recognition of her true vocation 'as a woman',

that she will now find true happiness in the world, as opposed to abandoning it for a convent, (see below) since there is not a shred of evidence for this in the script. If Isabella turns to the Duke 'with a heavenly and yielding smile' (see Lawrence 1931, pp. 106–7) she may well do it to serve the plot, and not to point a moral about the nature of ideal womanhood that makes her kneeling and yielding so wonderful to certain male critics. I'd rather see Isabella turn to the Duke with a contemptuous sneer, simply *because* of the way certain commentators have made sexual (sexist?) mileage out of the breath-taking, heart-stopping impact of Isabella's having finally proved herself 'a woman' worthy of His Grace, the Duke:

> [Isabella may] be seen as successfully undergoing a test which proves her worthy of marriage to the Duke.... Seen against the tradition to which Isabella belongs, her marriage to the Duke is inevitable from the start.
>
> (Lavin 1972, p. 109)

> [The Duke involves Isabella] intimately with Mariana, a woman whose sexual desires are at once open and legitimate.... Mariana wants her man, and far from being a scandal, it is an education for Isabella to help her get him. [Isabella's plea] in behalf of the man she thinks executed her brother ... is made possible precisely because her recognition of herself as a woman has taught her the human need for mercy. Her sexual awareness is not vanity, it is humility.... The Duke's proposal offers the promise that in marriage Isabella can fully express her newborn awareness of herself as a woman.
>
> (Kirsch 1975, pp. 97, 100)

> [Because] kings and dukes are petty earthly gods, the glory Isabella derives from her regal marriage reflects the true glory that consists in the good will of God.... Her

'comforts' have about them an aura of divinity, and they result, quite literally, from a purgative 'despair'....
Isabella's marriage also confirms her rejection of monastic bondage and the puerile good intentions that had led her into it. In every way, then, the wedding is a fitting conclusion for a plot that endeavours throughout to lead its principal actors from ... contentions bred of the flesh and the letter, to the tranquil joy that follows love's true essence.

(Gless 1979, pp. 213, 255)

[Isabella has learned] that the world has need for her; her life is still a consecrated life; the vital energy of her heart can exert and augment itself through glad and faithful wifehood, and through noble station more fully than in seclusion.

(Dowden 1875, p. 84)

[In the Royal Shakespeare Company production directed by Barry Kyle in 1978] Isabella's goal was the realisation of the warm-blooded woman hidden beneath her habit. At times her femininity [sic] broke out in moments of petulant anger, impotently kicking a pile of prisoners' clothes, or wild despair, tearing off her veil and rosary on hearing that her brother was dead. She was drawn to the Duke by his newly discovered confidence and charm and by their mutual excitement in the plan to trap Angelo. In the pleasure she got from the intrigue Miss Dionisotti became an engaging heroine, giggling as she mapped out with straw the scene of Mariana's assignation in Angelo's garden. When the Duke eventually proposed marriage her reaction was so enthusiastic that his second proposal was cut from the text, and his response 'But fitter time for that' [5.1. 490] to this passionate young woman carried the knowing smile which suggested a cooling-off period before enthusiastic love-making.

(Nicholls 1986, pp. 79–80)

By contrast, I have yet to find a comparable series of critical allelulias and hosannas proclaiming that the Duke's proposals to Isabella reflect his new-born awareness of the 'warm-blooded' man beneath the friar's habit and the robes of stage; that his bosom is, now, *truly* 'complete'; that the vital energy of his heart can, at last, exert and augment itself through glad and faithful husbandhood; and that, in middle age, he will find his noble station in life newly consecrated by marriage to a lovely young virgin, and so on and so forth.

There could be good reasons why critics who write about Isabella in terms of her emergent 'femininity' do not write in comparable, lip-smacking, terms about the Duke's ‑'masculinity'. For a man who, 'above all other strifes, contended especially to know himself' (III.ii. 218), the Duke seems not to have known that his 'complete bosom' was *not* invulnerable to the dribbling dart of love, unless—could it be?—a due sincerity governed his insistence that he 'was not inclin'd that way', until *he* looked on Isabella. There is, therefore, one structural parallel that critics who extol the ending often tend to ignore: what the Duke's proposal does do, structurally at least, is to associate (even as it contrasts the honourable and dishonourable nature of their proposals) the Duke with the other man in the play who was not, previously, 'much detected for women' until the 'lovely' self of the same 'virtuous maid' subdued him quite:

> *Angelo*   ... Ever till now,
>   When men were fond, I smil'd and wond'red
>   how.

$$\text{(II.ii. 186–7)}$$

The Duke's cousin, Angelo, is the character on stage who most eloquently articulates the comparable critical insistence (desire?) that Isabella must, finally and 'fully', express 'her newborn awareness of herself as a woman' by putting on the 'destin'd livery':

> *Angelo*   ... Be that you are,
> That is, a woman; if you be more, you're none;
> If you be one, as you are well express'd
> By all external warrants, show it now
> By putting on the destin'd livery.
>
>   (II.iv. 134–8)

As Jacqueline Rose has observed, in these lines Angelo 'states most clearly the *more* and the *less* that woman becomes when she fails to contain for the man the sexuality which she provokes' (Rose 1985, p.97).

There are, of course, various reasons why the structural parallels between the way the dart of love for the same young novice pierced the hitherto invulnerable bosoms of the Duke and Angelo alike, are very seldom mentioned in critical interpretations of Isabella's heavenly and yielding responses to the Duke. One obvious reason is that to stress the parallels might make the Duke's honourable intentions, and Angelo's dishonourable intentions, seem comparably lascivious and lurid. Yet it is no more—*or less*—absurd to argue that the Duke, as 'a man', is blood-cousin to Angelo, than it is to argue that Isabella has gained a 'new-born awareness of herself as a woman' through association with Mariana. Moreover, unless the parallels are taken into account, the Duke's proposal seems as inconsistent with *his* previous behaviour and motivation as an acceptance of it seems inconsistent with Isabella's. But then, perhaps they *are* equally inconsistent. It could be argued that both the Duke's proposal, and Isabella's acceptance of it, were mandated by the playwright's need to tie-up his plot and make sure that its comic resolution will encompass the hero and heroine; and so the Duke and Isabella lead Angelo and Mariana and Claudio and Julietta in the exit-wedding march—that is, unless you interpret the proposal and acceptance allegorically, and see the wedding of the Duke and Isabella as a symbolic union of his 'Grace' with her 'Virtue', *both* of which have, previously, been shown to be incomplete without the other (I am indebted for this argument to a paper by Evert Sprinchorn).

Throughout *Measure for Measure* an allegorical, or symbolic, level of action and meaning seems underscored by the biblical echoes and the conceptual associations stressed in the names and titles of various characters, even as the line Isabella addresses to Angelo, 'Save your honour!', carries more weight than an honorific address to a judge (see Mahood 1957, p.179, and Schleiner 1982, pp.227–35). There are puns on the names of Angelo (Angel, Coin), Escalus (Scales, Stair + social ladder?), and Lucio (Light, Lucifer?) as well as on the names of Abhorson, Pompey Bum, Elbow, Froth, Kate Keepdown and Mistress Overdone. Other associations appear to lurk behind the lines: is the Duke a figure of God the Father; a Christ figure; or the figure of a god who lets a cruel archangel punish sinners for him? Or is he a symbolic tribute to King James, and the play itself a tribute to the king's own treatise on the properties of government, the *Basilicon Doron*? Or what you will? One could argue that if we try to incorporate *all* these associations into some overall interpretation of the play, then all the incorporation and interpreting (like Fluellen's triumphant demonstration that Henry V and Alexander the Great were alike because their realms both contained rivers, and 'there is salmons in both') appears to be our work—not Shakespeare's (see Levin 1979, pp.209–29). If, uncertain how to justify the intervention of his *deus ex machina*, and unable to resolve the problems posed in the first acts without doing so, Shakespeare riddled his text with *non sequiturs*, contradictory moral attitudes, impressive-sounding references to Power Divine, and elaborate in-jokes to compliment King James, then we shall have great difficulty in finding out exactly what Shakespeare wants us to understand. We shall have to reason it out much as we reason out a notice in some language we are not fully familiar with. Thus, some pretty strenuous reasoning may be interposed between the author's portrayals of the characters and actions and our interpretation of them, and it is strangely easy to forget that all the reasoning and interpreting was not Shakespeare's, but our own. Yet there is no denying that the riddled, allusive, language of the play itself suggests alternative ways of interpreting the symbolism—and the realism—involved in its construction and characterisation alike.

For instance, more than a century ago Gervinus declared that the play's basic moral concern was with the idea of moderation as applied to all human relationships (see Lever 1965, p. lix). Throughout the play, extremes give rise to their opposites—'Too much liberty' gives rise to 'restraint', etc.—in ways which suggest that this may be a basic structural principle of the tragi-comedy as a whole:

> It calls us universally from all extremes, even from that of the good, because in every extreme there lies an overstraining, which avenges itself with the contrary reaction.
>
> (Gervinus [1875], 1971, p. 504)

However you interpret the moral of *Measure for Measure*, it seems demonstrably true that differing theses give rise to their antitheses, as it were in a kind of dramatic dialectic, or through the operation of this tragi-comedy's first, and second, laws of dramatic thermodynamics. Muriel Bradbrook thus compares the 'inward and outward actions of the play' to Ptolemaic spheres 'enclosed within each other, moving in contrary directions':

> The outer world reflects back upon man that aspect with which he confronts it, so that measure for measure is the law of relation between man and man, but the retributive powers of the world are complemented by diabolic or angelic impulses from within the heart of each man, so that Isabella calls out lust unknown to himself in Angelo, the Duke by apparently satisfying his desire calls out an

impulse to murder. Mariana, whose earthly hopes had been destroyed by her brother's death, calls out in Isabella an impulse of compassion, which expresses itself in legalistic terms. Thus the two spheres join in her final plea.

(Bradbrook 1982, p. 153)

Regardless of whether you conclude that the fusion of the play's inward and outer action, or of its literal and symbolic levels of action, is or is not successfully accomplished in the end, this seems a useful way of looking at the structure. Taken literally, the Duke's proposal to Isabella—

> if you'll a willing ear incline,
> What's mine is yours, and what is yours is mine.
>
> (V.i. 534–5)

—seems right in there with 'I could be happy with you,/If you could be happy with me' in the tritest proposal of the centuries contest. On the other hand, it *could* be used to support Bradbrook's argument that when the Duke thus 'offers a share of his power' to Isabella,

This is not a wooing but a species of coronation; perhaps as Angelo might be physically stripped of the insignia of judge and of a noble (he is the Duke's cousin, apparently his next of kin), so perhaps Isabel should receive the coronet or the sceptre that honours Truth'.

(Bradbrook 1982, p. 153)

You could also see it as a joining of, an investment of, Grace with Virtue, and Virtue with Grace. Yet the Duke's lines themselves still sound so banal that they virtually have to be invested with allegorical significance if they are to be critically extolled as profoundly meaningful rather than purely perfunctory.

By somewhat the same token, the Duke's disguise as a friar simply has to be seen as a symbolic vestment associating him with divine benevolence, or divine omniscience; otherwise, his behaviour, so disguised, might well seem, to Protestants, to be typical of the nefarious behaviour of Catholic friars that Burton so vehemently deplored. It would, moreover, seem even more offensive to Catholics:

> To assume a holy habit, and power of absolving sins which he did not possess, to hear confession (5. 1. 525) and to betray secrets of the confessional given to himself (3. 1. 165) and to others (4. 3. 125) is so monstrous that a Spanish censor has simply cut the whole play out of the Folio in a copy at Valladolid.
>
> (Bradbrook 1952, p.147)

Discussing the play's portrayal of Catholicism, E. A. J. Honigmann (1985, p.123) asks whether a Protestant audience would have 'sympathized with a friar who takes it upon himself to play the role of "power divine"'. 'The Duke-as-friar, confessor to Angelo, takes advantage of his disguise to intrigue incessantly, trying to make rings round those who trust him—very much as Catholic priests played games with other men's lives according to Protestant propaganda.' For that matter, 'Isabella's willingness to go along with the friar's proposed bed-trick, after she had so roundly condemned the cohabitation of Claudio and Juliet—an inconsistency that has puzzled many commentators—might well be viewed, by a Protestant audience, as another example of Catholic authoritarianism: a novice *must* suppress her conscience when a "good father" orders her to.' And, of course, 'the play's Catholic ramifications ... (Isabella's wish to be a nun; the "friar", and his officious meddling)' were Shakespeare's additions to the story. Although the play is not overtly anti-Catholic, Honigmann concludes that it does 'activate latent anti-Catholic feeling—while at the same time it manages to present a Catholic point of view persuasively from the inside.' In any case, when looked at literally, the Duke's behaviour as a friar might seem equally reprehensible to Protestants and Catholics alike. Yet it could be that the sinister side of Shakespeare's Duke of dark corners is what makes him so much more interesting than the ingratiating bungler, or the Heavenly-Father-Figure (to whom we should all sing critical hosannas), who emerges from certain critical interpretations of the play. But then, in drama, I personally tend to prefer—as advertisements for Erich von Stroheim's films put it—the kind of 'Man You Love To Hate' to the kind of man you hate, but whom you are told you must (or are officially supposed to) love.

When it is looked at on a symbolic level, *Measure for Measure* may, in turn, be compared to, or contrasted with, a morality play. Looked at on a literal level, it can be as easily compared to, or contrasted with, works of altogether different genres (novels, problem-plays, operas, operettas—see the Appendix below). For instance, there is one very popular form of drama today wherein new characters are arbitrarily introduced, new complications devised, and characters who behave in one way in one episode subsequently alter their behaviour in accordance with the script-writer's immediate purpose; that is, the soap-opera. And if the action of *Measure for Measure* foreshadows the action of a grand opera, like *Tosca*, its episodic, cliff-hanging, mission-impossible structure (how are the characters going to get of *this* mess?) has equally obvious features in common with that of a popular soap-opera, like *Dallas*: 'Come to my bed', said J.R. to Sue Ellen in one episode, 'or I'll have your young and innocent lover sent to jail on a drug-charge'. Indeed, nothing could be easier than to chart comparable cliff-hanging episodes in the continuing saga of *Vienna*:

Episode 1. Will Isabella yield to Angelo? If not, will Claudio die? Episode 2. Will the bed-trick succeed? If so, will Angelo pardon Claudio? Episode 3. Since Angelo breaks his word and refuses to pardon Claudio, how will the Duke save poor Claudio from the executioner's axe? Will he allow Barnardine to die? Episode 4. When will the Duke make his power known? Will Isabella pardon Angelo for Mariana's sake? Will the Duke really have Lucio whipped and hanged? Will Isabella accept the Duke's proposal? And so on and on: Will Isabella find true happiness as a Duchess? Will Mariana find happiness with Angelo? Although the action of *Measure for Measure* is condensed into three hours, and that of a soap-opera can be extended *ad infinitum*, it is probably best to play each episode and each character in *Measure for Measure*, for maximum dramatic impact, as they would be portrayed in a soap-opera. After all, its dramatic life may well depend on its sensational, lurid, suspenseful qualities. It is easy to sneer at students and critics who write about the characters and situations in *Measure for Measure* as if they were writing about a soap-opera, or to put them down for writing in a 'noveletty' way. But the play does have its 'noveletty' features, and a structure comparable to the episodic novels ('Will little Nell die?') from which the structure of the soap-opera descended to keep audiences coming back for more today. For that matter, at least so far as I know, Shakespeare himself never appears to have been dramatically inhibited by critical considerations of due decorum and good taste. And it could be that the affinities, *not the lack of affinities*, between Shakespearian drama and popular genres such as romances and revenge-plays, and novels and soap-operas account, today as yesterday, for their primary appeal to an audience. But of course they have other qualities as well.

Here, for what they are worth, are my own conclusions about the relationship between the literal and symbolic forms of characterisation in *Measure for Measure*. It seems to me that the critical dichotomy between dramatic realism and symbolism is a false one. The conflicts and characters involved in the greatest of all realistic plays—those of Ibsen and Chekhov and Strindberg, for example—always have symbolic overtones, and the greatest of symbolic plays always place some real toads within their imaginary gardens. As Yeats reminds us in a poem appropriately entitled 'The Circus Animals' Desertion', it is a fatal mistake to assume that even the most masterful images of art have their ultimate origins in, or make their primary impact on, 'pure mind', or that they can long survive independently of their energy sources in, and the powerlines leading up from and down to, the place where all artistic ladders start, in the 'foul rag-and-bone shop of the heart'. Artists such as Yeats and Brecht and Marianne Moore, whose work could not be more different in other respects, alike stress the rawness of the raw materials of art. 'I, too, dislike it', said Marianne Moore of the technical contrivances involved in art: 'there are things that are important beyond all this fiddle'. She goes on (in a poem entitled 'Poetry') to plead for genuineness, for rawness,

> Nor till the poets among us can be
>   'literalists of
>   the imagination'—above
>   insolence and triviality and can present
>   for inspection, 'imaginary gardens with real toads in
>   them',
>   shall we have it.

It seems to me that the organic life in Measure for Measure, or, if you will, the 'lot of raw materials Shakespeare shovels onto the stage', or the real toads in this imaginary garden, and the literal nature of its creator's imagination, are what account for its primary impact.

Yet the symbolic reverberations of the play give everything in it the kind of 'astonishing, wondrous aspect' described by Robertson Davies (in his novel about theatrical magic, *World of Wonders*), even as the ubiquitous, strangely omniscient Duke seems to represent the power behind the scenes, the forces on which the drama symbolically depends. Davies describes the strange sense of apprehension and recognition we have of 'the Great Justice and the Great Mercy whenever they choose to make themselves known' in a way that might serve as a gloss on Act 5 of *Measure for Measure*:

> '... I don't monkey with what I think of as the Great Justice—'
> 'Poetic justice,' said Liesl.
> 'What you please. Though it doesn't look poetic in action. It's rough and tough and deeply satisfying. And I don't administer it. Something else—something that I don't understand, but feel and serve and fear—does that. It's sometimes horrible to watch, as it was when my poor, deal old master, Sir John, was brought down by his own vanity and Milady went with him.... But part of the glory and terror of our life is that somehow, at some time, we get all that's coming to us.'
>
>   (Davies 1983, pp.861–2)

There is a sense of a 'Great Mercy' in operation at the end of *Measure for Measure*, yet there is also a 'Great Justice' administered by something we may not understand, but 'feel' and 'fear', whereby the Duke gives certain characters *just* what they have coming to them: the libertine, Lucio, is forced to marry the whore he got with the child he abandoned; Angelo, like it or lump it, has to lie down in the second-best bed of Mariana. Its operation may seem painful (if not 'horrible') to watch, in so far as the general situation in Duke Vincentio's Vienna seems a set-up comparable to the ultimate practical joke:

> Forgive, O Lord, my little jokes on Thee
> And I'll forgive Thy great big one on me.
>
>   (Robert Frost, 'In the Clearing')

Yet it also has its 'deeply satisfying', 'astonishing, wonderous aspects' of the kind summed up in the immortal 'Goody-Goody!' (by Johnny Mercer and Matt Malneck):

> Hooray and hallelujah!
> You had it comin' to ya!

And it is ultimately associated with Shakespeare's great mercy as well: as is the Duke who is its administrator.

So far as characterisation is concerned, in the drama (as in life) symbolism and realism come together inasmuch as the most remarkable individuals we encounter on, or off, the stage, are those who seem to stand for, or to symbolise, something: whether that something be temporal or spiritual power, the will to know, or sheer anarchic energy, or incorrigible pomposity, gullibility or greed. This is why Dr Johnson said that Shakespeare's greatest characters seem representative of a whole 'species' of humankind. Falstaff, for instance, is Elizabethan drama's King of Carnival and Lord of Misrule. Cleopatra is associated with the powers of the Goddess Venus and the Goddess Isis. In *Measure for Measure*, as elsewhere (everywhere?) in the greatest plays by Shakespeare, it is as if the playwright limits the number of major characters in correspondence with the number of forces which contend on the psychological level, even as the seemingly fortuitous events in the play are designed to trigger latent forces in the persons whom they effect (see Thurman 1982, pp. 382–3). Thus, Isabella's account of Angelo's proposition to her, as it were inadvertently, triggers Claudio's will to live—a force subsequently extinguished in Claudio by the Duke, but considered important enough to be reasserted, by Shakespeare, in Barnardine's defiance of the Duke: 'I will not consent to die this day, that's certain' (IV.iii. 52). Likewise, Isabella's virtue triggers Angelo's lust, and so on (for other examples, see Bradbrook as quoted above). To my mind, anyway, the reason why the individual characters here portrayed elicit such passionately partisan responses from differing critics, and students, and members of the audience, is that the same psychological forces that contend with each other on stage, also contend with each other, and trigger comparable reactions, in *us*.

It seems to me that any audience at *Measure for Measure* (whether Jacobean or modern) is very likely to include some people who share some (or most) of the qualities portrayed, both positively and negatively, within the play itself. There is, for instance, in some of us, as in Isabella, a spirit prepared to sacrifice everything, including life, in order to maintain its own chastity (or integrity or autonomy) inviolate. But there is also, in many of us, a cringing Claudio prepared to sacrifice our own honour or integrity, and to let anyone else sacrifice what they believe to be their honour or integrity— only 'let me live'. Angelo is not the only person who ever lived who has desired to 'raze the sanctuary' and pitch his own evil there. Nor is he the only person whose 'sense' is more betrayed by woman's (or man's) 'virtue' than by 'lightness'. And there is an Angelo in lots of us who, having ourselves succumbed to a given temptation, wants other people—especially those who insist on maintaining their virtue—to follow us in the fall. There is a Lucio in some of us who likes to sling mud at authority-figures, to insist that they are no better than they should be (or than we are), like a private-eye seeing through their pretentions to moral superiority, as well as a Lucio-like tendency towards social, moral and sexual irresponsibility. Many of us also feel a need—a need by no means exclusive to women—for some authority, some Duke, who will tell us what to do, and who will solve our problems for us and absolve us from our sins. And there is a Duke in many of us who likes to exert power, to test, to sit in judgement, and then to extend our gracious benevolence and mercy to our students or our children. And for some of us it is easier to forgive a Barnardine (who murdered somebody we do not know) than to pardon a Lucio who personally insulted or slandered *us*. None of these are especially endearing traits. Nineteenth-century critics tended to complain that not one of the major characters in this play is particularly lovable, or even like-able. Twentieth-century defenders of the play, especially those who interpret it as morally exemplary, have, conversely, tended—depending on which character or form of behaviour they believe should be seen as exemplary—to accentuate the positive traits of, say, the Duke or Isabella in such a way as to eliminate the negative. Perhaps significantly, however, the word most strongly associated with 'guiltiness' (of all kinds) in this particular play is 'natural'. Indeed, it would seem unnatural *not* to be guilty of one or more of the vices here portrayed.

There is, for instance, one vice that most of us do most deplore, and most desire should meet the blow of justice (when we see it manifested in others): and that is a lack of charity *towards* the vices of others. Yet most of us will, quite naturally, succumb to the temptation to sin in loving the moral or dramatic virtues we are critically extolling to the degree that we prove guilty of an Angelo-like, Isabella-like, lack of charity in pitilessly castigating those characters whose vices we do not believe that we, or that morally enlightened members of the audience, actually do, or are supposed to share: including, paradoxically, a lack of charity.

> Hard as an icicle [Isabella] visits Claudio in prison and lays before him the terms and her decision.... because of her very inhumanity she can watch unmoved while he faces the awful realization of immediate death, her pitilessness only growing with his pleading. Weak as he is, his self-indulgence cannot stand comparison with hers, with the pitiless, unimaginative self-absorbed virtue which sustains her.
>
> (Ellis-Fermor 1936, p.262)

Thus a (comparatively) sympathetic response to Claudio

almost inevitably involves a (comparatively) pitiless attack on Isabella's 'pitilessness', even as a moral defence of Character Y almost invariably involves a moral or critical attack on Character X, as well as an attack on critical detractors of Character Y. Here, for instance, is a moral attack on critical detractors of Isabella:

> Let there be no mistake about this: Shakespeare sets up Isabella as a heroine, [whose chastity] represents something in womanhood which Shakespeare, no less than Lucio in this play, reveres with all his heart. Nothing but a pseudo-romantic sentimentalism, utterly alien to the spirit of Shakespeare and of Elizabethan England, could fail to understand the rightness of Isabella.... What we are pleased to call enlightenment to-day seeks to evade the embarrassing notion of sin, and is naturally anxious to enrol Shakespeare among its adepts. But sin, and deadly sin at that, is fundamental in Christian thought
>
> (Sisson 1934, p.58)

And here is a critical case against moral detractors of Claudio:

> Claudio is portrayed by Shakespeare with unfailing sympathy and affection. It is astonishing to find Coleridge describe him as 'detestable' and to hear other critics join in the chorus of abuse.
>
> (Schanzer 1963, p.80)

Likewise, as Kenneth Muir and Stanley Wells have observed,

> With *Measure for Measure* the controversy has sometimes been acrimonious between those who regard it as Shakespeare's most Christian play and those who think it cynical. The difficulty here is that each article on the play

published in *Shakespeare Survey* has been followed by an indignant rejoinder. The opening pages of a number of recent articles have been devoted to a summary of the damnable errors they seek to confute.... Indeed,the impression we get ... is that more than one interpretation can be based squarely on the text, not because of a failure of communication ... but rather because [the] ambiguity is a sign that Shakespeare's mind, in Keats's phrase, was 'a thoroughfare for all thoughts, not a select party'

(Muir and Wells 1982, pp. ix–x)

For that matter, one could argue that the fact that virtually every major character in the play has aroused comparably fervent responses (pro and con) testifies to the astonishing vitality of Shakespeare's imaginary beings. Thus, the passionate adoration which individual critics accord to their very own enskied and sainted Isabellas, and the equally passionate revulsion which other critics express towards their own smug, vixenish, intolerant, selfish Isabellas, alike testify to the fiery, icy Isabella's extra-dramatic life-everlasting in the heavens or hells assigned to her by individual imaginations.

So far as the dramatic forgiveness of sins, and the life-everlasting, are concerned, it could be argued that, even as Shakespeare encourages us to grant pardon to the *most* sinister character portrayed on the stage in this particular play (contrast, for instance, his portrayal of the utterly unsympathetic Cornwall in *King Lear*), he likewise extends his mercy to every *other* character here portrayed. If we can pardon *Angelo*, we can, *mutatis mutandis*, pardon everyone else, including each other, and ourselves, along with Angelo, the Duke, Isabella, Lucio, Claudio, Julietta and Barnardine. The obvious reason why we can argue a strong case for charity towards all and malice towards none, is that (I'm paraphrasing *Othello*, V.ii. 345–6), although Shakespeare himself nothing extenuates, *neither* does he set down aught in malice. Nor is *Measure for Measure* the only play wherein Shakespeare gives his very devils their due measure of sympathy and understanding. 'This thing of darkness I/Acknowledge mine', says Prospero of Caliban, the prime representative of 'natural' guiltiness in *The Tempest* (V.i. 275–6). And Prospero's line raises the interesting question, 'Whose *are* Shakespeare's things of darkness if *not* his?' By giving a measure of understanding, and sympathy, as well as his final forgiveness, to the characters whose paths he, himself, beset with the very traps and pitfalls they fell into, Shakespeare (unlike?—or like?— the Duke) would seem to show a kind of divinely humane compassion for their suffering and guilt. I realise that these, as well as various other, arguments may be anathematised, by the post-structuralist left and the radical right alike, as manifest examples of a 'liberal humanist' appropriation of Shakespeare. And one could, of course, argue the opposite case: Shakespeare may here be attempting to do what Sir Philip Sidney (in his *Apology for Poetry*) insisted the comic playwright ought to do; and that is to present his comic figures of common vices and follies and errors in 'the most ridiculous and scornful way what may be, so as it is impossible that any beholder can be content to be such a one'. But that argument, in effect, eliminates the positive— the compassion and understanding and generosity—that pervades the play's tragi-comic treatment of erring humanity.

It seems to me that, if the balance of *Measure for Measure* is weighted at all, it is weighted on the side of a freedom that constitutes the ultimate charity; that is, on the side of the poet's freedom to accentuate both the positive and negative aspects of human virtue and of vice, as well as the playwright-actor's freedom to portray, with sympathy and understanding, the least sympathetic of human beings. Thus, the most problematical of all problem plays leaves us free to draw whatever conclusions we will from the 'examples' that Shakespeare here leaves, as it were, 'to operate by chance'. It is the critical (and directorial) dialectic, not the Shakespearian dialectic, that prohibits certain sympathetic (or hostile) responses to the individual characters. In this sense, the critical dialectic and the Shakespearian dialectic are at odds: precisely because Shakespeare issues no prohibitions whatsoever, the best critical, or moral, arguments ever posited by the most brilliant critic who ever lived, cannot prevent you, or me, or anyone else, from responding negatively, or positively, to say, Claudio or Isabella or the Duke. Indeed, the fact that equally   distinguished   commentators   have   posited comparably valid cases for the prosecution and the defence of virtually every character in the play would seem conclusive proof that Shakespeare left them—and leaves us—free to respond to his characters in altogether different ways, and indeed provides us with the alternative perspectives on the various characters and conflicts that inevitably result in alternating currents of reaction charged with equivalent emotional energy.

The play's peculiarly modern relevance may be the result of Shakespeare's tendency to confront us with moral and dramatic conundrums; to stack the deck, then shuffle it; to let his witnesses plead their own cases; and to let the evidence speak for itself. He thus looses the positive and negative forces of sexuality and morality, of vice and virtue, of authority and anarchy, to fight it out with each other, on the stage, and in our own minds, just as they do on their old prize-fighting stage, the world. This is why, to critics from Morgann to Brecht, Shakespeare appeared to have shovelled the raw materials of life itself onto the stage: like those halls-of-mirrors simultaneously affording differing (right-hand/left-hand) perspectives on the human figure, the dramatic mirrors that Shakespeare holds up to human nature never cease to reflect the real thing. Could Shakespeare be accurately described as the world's greatest behavioural psychologist? Is there any other author, past or present, from whose works we can learn, in anything like so short an amount of time, anything like so much about the astonishing range and variety of desires and needs and virtues and vices and forces and counter-forces that (today as yesterday) interact with each other to agitate, adorn or disgrace humankind? Of how many other authors could Lord Lyttelton's statement be made without seeming quite ridiculous?

> If human nature were destroyed, and no monument were left of it except [Shakespeare's] works, other beings might know *what man was* from those writings.
>
>   (Lyttelton, in Nicol Smith 1916, p. 73)

Some centuries later, Tallulah Bankhead's father arrived at a similar conclusion when he told his daughters that 'if they knew Shakespeare and the Bible and could shoot craps', that was all the education they were likely to need (Gill 1972, p. 21). Looked at from these angles, *Measure for Measure* takes its place among those works without which Lyttelton's 'other beings' would not know a measure of truth about the ways of our world and the strange and various species of humankind that have inhabited it. Nor, perhaps, would we.

But be that as it may. There is, perhaps, no other author from whom we can learn so much about the extraordinary range and variety of forces active in art. For instance, it is as if, in *Measure for Measure*, Shakespeare himself suggested all of the possible permutations (tragic and comic, symbolic and realistic, exalted and lurid, profound and profane) implicit in a single plot. Because successive artists (major and minor, and in works of very different kinds) have developed differing facets of the various moral, sexual and legal conflicts involved in the confrontations between Angelo, Isabella and Claudio, I have attached an Appendix on the 'Legacy' of *Measure for Measure*: partly because some of the variants are so amusing, and partly because, by paying very different forms of tribute to *Measure for Measure* than critics have paid it, subsequent works of art may, retroactively, illuminate the dramatic forces and counter-forces involved in Shakespeare's original portrayals of the confrontations between Isabella, Angelo and Claudio themselves.

Appendix
The Legacy

The Sources

The major sources for *Measure for Measure* have been discussed so well, by J. W. Lever, Mark Eccles and Kenneth Muir (among others) that only a few points about them need be reiterated here. His sources for the 'monstrous ransom' plot offered Shakespeare a multiple choice of ways to present, and resolve, the conflicts between Isabella, Angelo and Claudio. In several prose versions of the conflict (see Lever 1965, pp. xxvii, 151–4), Claudio's counterpart is the husband, not the brother, of Isabella's counterpart. When the corrupt judge breaks his promise to spare her husband's life if she yields to him, the heroine appeals to the Duke's counterpart for justice. He orders the villain to marry the heroine, so saving her honour while investing her with the villain's wealth, and then orders the villain's execution. This ending leaves the heroine with the satisfaction of having had revenge/justice, along with a dowry sufficient to attract a new husband if she wants one. Compare the Duke's lines to Mariana:

> Consenting to the safeguard of your honour,
> I thought your marriage fit; else imputation,
> For that he knew you, might reproach your life,

128

And choke your good to come. For his possessions,
Although by confiscation they are ours,
We do instate and widow you withal,
To buy you a better husband.

(V.i. 417–23)

In Shakespeare's dramatic sources, like Whetstone's
Promos and Cassandra, the heroine, like Isabella, is sister to
the man condemned. In these versions, the corrupt
magistrate yet again reneges on his promise, and orders the
brother executed, but Claudio's counterpart is rescued by a
sympathetic jailer. The heroine appeals to the Duke's
counterpart for justice: he orders the villain to marry the
heroine, then orders his execution. But the heroine
subsequently decides, like Mariana, to stand by her
husband, and implores mercy from the Duke's counterpart,
while the villain is shown to feel genuine love for the woman
he had so grievously betrayed. The brother, who had been
in disguise, reveals himself and all ends happily: 'The lost
sheepe founde, for joye, the feast was made' (see *Promos and
Cassandra*, II.v. 6, reprinted in Eccles 1980, p. 369).

Shakespeare may, or may not, have known exactly how
he was going to resolve the conflicts when he started writing
Measure for Measure, but he was obviously aware of the
alternative emotional currents, towards revenge, towards
temporal justice, towards reconciliation, towards Christian
mercy, interacting in his sources. The most dramatic
changes he made to the earlier versions are equally obvious:
(1) He initially raises the sexual stakes by making his heroine
a young novice. (2) The bed-trick is his way of subsequently
lowering the sexual stakes by substituting the maidenhead
of Angelo's old fiancée, Mariana, for the maidenhead of a
novice; thus Shakespeare simultaneously preserves
Isabella's 'sacred chastity' and Mariana's honour (by
marrying Angelo to Mariana) whilst bringing Angelo to
justice. (3) In none of the sources is the Duke's counterpart

involved in the action as the 'monstrous ransom' situation develops.

Seen in terms of the sources, Shakespeare's treatment of the conflicts would seem to contain, or suggest, alternative courses of action, as it were in the process of rejecting them, even as the Duke suggests, although he does not intend, that Angelo, in justice, ought to be denied, not granted, the mercy he himself denied to Claudio (V.i. 405–13). For another instance, the fact that Angelo orders the execution after the bed-trick clearly implies that, without intervention from some external agency, Claudio would have been killed whether Isabella had yielded to Angelo or not. And had Isabella actually been violated, then betrayed (this alternative possibility is posited as a trap for Angelo in V.i. 92–103), the ending would indeed have baffled her strong, indignant cries for 'justice, justice, justice, justice' (V.i. 25). What is of interest here is that the alternative courses of action involved have such great potential for dramatic development. Therefore, as we shall see, conflicts analogous to the ones between Isabella, Angelo and Claudio have tended to arise, with the regularity of Count Dracula, in later works of altogether different kinds.

Some Theatrical Permutations

The only performance of *Measure for Measure* clearly recorded in Shakespeare's lifetime is the one at the banqueting house in Whitehall on 26 December 1604. Although it was written at about the same time Shakespeare wrote *Othello*, when he was at the height of his powers, *Measure for Measure* does not emerge, from extant contemporary records, as one of his most popular plays. Cuts and prompter's notes in a copy of the First Folio in the University of Padua suggest that it might have been marked for a performance sometime between 1640 and 1660 (see Eccles 1980, p. 468), but there is no other record of an actual production until after the Restoration.

In 1660, Sir William Davenant, who took pride in letting people believe that he might have been Shakespeare's illegitimate son, was granted a warrant to act 'Measures, for Measures', along with eight other plays by Shakespeare. But what Davenant's company actually performed, on 15 February 1662, was his own adaptation of the play; and *The Law Against Lovers* could well constitute the best possible evidence that Sir William may indeed have been Shakespeare's bastard son. *The Law Against Lovers* begins pretty much as *Measure for Measure* does. The Duke leaves Angelo in charge of law and order in Vienna. But interwoven with the Angelo–Claudio–Isabella plot is the Beatrice-and-Benedick plot imported from *Much Ado About Nothing* (Benedick is Angelo's brother), while Beatrice's young sister, Viola (later destined to star in *Twelfth Night?*) is brought in to sing some new songs. The 'monstrous ransom' situation develops apace: Angelo says he will have Claudio executed if Isabella does not yield to him. But, in the meantime, Angelo's tyranny sparks a revolution led by the dashing Benedick. The revolutionaries storm the prison and release Claudio, and then imprison Angelo. Isabella goes to see Angelo in jail and finds him in a state of abject remorse, and more in love with her than ever: 'Because she doubts my virtue I must die,/Who did with vitious acts her virtue try'. For Davenant's Angelo never really intended to take Isabella against her will (Davenant got this idea from *Measure for Measure*, III.i. 160–9), he was only testing her virtue, which he found wondrous beyond all measure. Nor did he ever really intend to execute Claudio:

> Keep still your virtue, which is dignify'd
> And has new value got by being try'd.
> Claudio shall live longer than I can do,
> Who was his Judge, but am condemned by you.
> The martial of the Guards keeps secretly
> His pardon seal'd; nor meant I he should die.

Given his love of virtue, this Angelo indeed seems the right man for Isabella. And so, when the Duke manifests his power and pardons everyone in the end, the wedding bells peal joyously for Isabella and Angelo, Beatrice and Benedick, Claudio and Julietta alike. Thus Davenant eliminates all the problems caused by the bed-trick, and all the incongruities involved in the pairing off of the young novice, Isabella, with the paternalistic Duke. He thus files off the play's fangs and leaves a smooth smile. But it is interesting that he saw Isabella and Angelo, not Isabella and the Duke, as soul-mates.

In 1700, Charles Gildon's new adaptation, *Measure for Measure, or Beauty the Best Advocate*, was acted with an all-star cast. Shakespeare's play was radically cut to allow the interpolation of 'Dido and Aeneas', a masque with music by Henry Purcell. Gildon's Angelo emphasises the connections between the situations in the masque and the play when he proclaims his most nefarious intentions towards Isabella: 'And when, my Dido, I've possess'd thy charms,/I then will throw thee from my glutted arms'. Gildon's Angelo and Mariana, like his Claudio and Julietta, were not just betrothed, but secretly married. Thus Gildon stresses the legality of the sexual relationship between Claudio and Julietta, and underscores the justice involved in the bed-trick, since his Angelo had not only jilted a fiancée, but tried to deny an actual wedding for mercenary reasons.

The first recorded performance of Shakespeare's own *Measure for Measure* since 1604 occurred 116 years later, on 8 December 1720. 'The acting version printed for Tonson in 1722 keeps all Shakespeare's characters with cuts mainly in 1.2 and 2.1, and adds only eight lines, at the end' (Eccles 1980, p.469). But theatrical adaptations of *Measure for Measure* did not stop there. 'Between 1931 and 1934 Bertolt Brecht converted *Measure for Measure* into *Die Rundköpfe und die Spitzköpfe* (*Round Heads and Pointed Heads*), a Marxist allegory in which the Duke becomes a Viceroy who represents capitalism, while Angelo becomes Angelo Iberin, a deputy who represents Adolf Hitler' (see Watts 1986, p. 132). Moreover, as Watts also observes, certain recent productions should, in honesty, have been advertised 'as a director's free adaptation, or as a new play "based on" *Measure for Measure*, rather than as Shakespeare's play' (p. 113). Surely Brecht's—or Gildon's or Davenant's—adaptation would have been preferable to the inane travesty of the play I saw performed by the Royal Shakespeare Company at Stratford in 1978, wherein Angelo was portrayed as if he were Malvolio (imported from *Twelfth Night*): Isabella looked and acted like the head-girl in an English public school; and Mariana was introduced to the audience as a lush, swilling her booze directly from the bottle, on the haystack at the moated grange. For a fuller account of the way Isabella was portrayed in this production, see Graham Nicholls (1986, pp. 79–80), quoted above on p. 108.

Musical Permutations

Even as Davenant turned *Measure for Measure* into a kind of operetta, Gilbert and Sullivan subsequently recycled the 'law against lovers' in *The Mikado* (see Bradbrook 1982, and Bennett 1966, p. 158). Bradbrook also quotes the ending of Gilbert's first farce, *Trial by Jury*, with reference to the Duke's 'final award' to Isabella (quoted in Bradbrook 1982, p. 146):

> Barristers, and you, attorneys,
> Set out on your homeward journeys;
> . . . .
> Put your briefs upon the shelf,
> I will marry her myself!

In *My Life*, Richard Wagner tells how he adapted his opera, *Das Liebesverbot* (*The Ban on Love*) from *Measure for*

Measure: 'In his verse libretto he changed the plot so that Isabella rouses the people of Palermo to revolt against the viceroy and free Claudio from prison' (see Eccles 1980, pp.480–1). And, of course, the 'monstrous ransom' situation is the basis for Giaccomo Puccini's grand opera, *Tosca* (1900), wherein the villain, Scarpia, tells the heroine she can save her lover's life only by giving herself to him, and in exchange he will arrange a mock execution for her lover. Tosca agrees, but seeing a knife on Scarpia's table, seizes it and kills him. But Scarpia had tricked Tosca, and the execution of her lover is real. Distraught, she flings herself from the battlements of the Castel Sant' Angelo.

Novels, Short Stories, Memoirs

In *The Heart of Midlothian*, by Sir Walter Scott, the sister of the heroine is condemned to death for infanticide because she did not seek help with the birth of her illegitimate child. To save her sister, Jeanie Dean, a peasant girl of profound religious convictions, would have to lie about the delivery. She does not do so since lying, for her, constitutes a cardinal sin comparable to a nun's breaking of her vows of chastity. But she subsequently walks from Scotland to London to plead for pardon for her sister. The plot is finally resolved by a complex series of events vaguely comparable to the resolution to *Measure for Measure*, and the success of the resolution is, likewise, subject to critical debate.

In his short novel, *Billy Budd*, Herman Melville focuses on the predicament of a judge bound to enforce the rule of law even when the enforcement of it is manifestly unjust. In doing so, he provides a tragic gloss on certain legal and moral conundrums involved in *Measure for Measure*. Melville's Captain Vere is faced by the paradox that, as a result of having struck down the vicious, Iago-like Claggart, Billy Budd, 'the angel of God', must hang for causing the death of a superior officer. At the 'last Assizes', Vere says,

divine justice will acquit Billy. But in a navy threatened by
spreading mutiny, Vere decides that he must proceed under
the law of the Mutiny Act; and the reasons he gives for his
decision are the same reasons Angelo gives for sentencing
Claudio to death ('It is the law, not I, condemn your
brother./Were he my kinsman, brother, or my son,/It
should be thus with him': II.ii. 80–2): 'For suppose
condemnation to follow these present proceedings. Would
it be so much we ourselves that would condemn as it would
be martial law operating through us?' Ultimately, in this
story, 'the condemned man suffered less than he who mainly
had effected the condemnation'. Thus Melville stresses the
potentially tragic dilemma of an 'upright judge': Captain
Vere did love Billy as a son, but felt bound to uphold the
rule of law. Comparable questions about the rule of law are
raised in the first half of *Measure for Measure*, and then
evaded in the second half. None the less, when the Duke
gives pardon to everyone on the criminal docket at the end,
there may well be ghostly stage-whispers chorusing
'Remember me' from the cellarage: they come from the
reverberating echoes of the most eloquent arguments by the
Duke, Escalus and Angelo concerning precedence and the
rule of law that subsequently constitute the focal point of
Melville's tragedy.

In his short novel *Boule de Suif*, Guy de Maupassant uses
the 'monstrous ransom' plot to expose moral hypocrisy.
The heroine, an intensely patriotic young French prostitute,
is told by the Prussian commander at the border that unless
she sleeps with him he will hold her, and the group she is
travelling with, at the border until she does. The
'respectable' people in the group use every form of moral
blackmail to get her to yield. She does so, and is
subsequently treated like dirt by everyone in the group, and
so is violated by them as viciously as by the Prussian
commandant. Guy de Maupassant also raises the question
why, in order to save her own life, or anyone else's, it would
seem that 'a woman's only duty was the continual sacrifice,

the perpetual surrender of her body'? And this question
remains wide open in spite of changing concepts about
feminine—and masculine—honour.

As ideas about honour change, so do assumptions about
whether Isabella's successors, or Shakespeare's Isabella
herself, should, or should not, pay the ransom demanded.
Yet what is most interesting is that, in most cases, as in the
case of Isabella, the surrender of her body to the villain
would *not*, in fact, have saved the life of the person for whom
the sacrifice was made. What saves Shakespeare's Claudio,
and Whetstone's Andrugio, is the intervention of someone
else (a sympathetic jailer, the Duke). Apart from such
intervention, the execution would have taken place whether
the heroine had yielded or not, just as it does in *Tosca*. And
see also Bob Dylan's 'Seven Curses', where Old Reilly's
daughter gives herself to the judge to save her father, but, the
next morning, saw 'that hangin' branch a-bendin',/She saw
her father's body broken' and knew 'the judge had never
spoken'. Critical and moral arguments against Isabella for
her refusal to yield never take this fact into account: yet it
does seem a fact (in life as in art) that paying a ransom does
not guarantee the safe release of the hostage. The best
argument against the 'moral' argument that it is Isabella's, or
any other woman's, 'moral' duty to sacrifice her body (or
integrity or soul) to save another person's life is that the
odds are awfully good that her sacrifice will be made in vain.
Or will be held against her, as it was in the case of Boule de
Suif. Kenneth Muir cites *The Way Things Happen*, a play by
Clemence Dane, wherein the man saved from prison is
furious with the woman who has bought his freedom (see
Muir, in Geckle 1970, p. 17).

Thus you can read the variants of the 'monstrous ransom'
plot as variants on the same moral and sexual conundrums.
But you can also read them as reflections of changing
assumptions concerning what, if anything, does, or does
not, constitute a fate worse than death; that is, concerning
sacred honour. In a letter discussing changing social, sexual

and historical assumptions about feminine and masculine honour, Isak Dinesen (Karen Blixen) cites two different Scandinavian versions of the 'monstrous ransom' plot:

> In one of Blicher's stories the heroine is given the choice between her young brother's life and the sacrifice of her (womanly) honour to the enemy commander, and neither she nor her brother entertain a moment's doubt: it is his life that must be sacrificed. In a modern story, by Jakob Wassarmann, a Bolshevik officer gives a young lady the promise of sparing a company of refugees if she will come to his quarters at night; she hesitates no longer than Blicher's brother and sister, but replies: 'Yes, of course,—here I am.' I think there are very few young women whose conscience and moral sense would not bid them give the same answer. For they no longer feel their 'womanliness' to be the most sacred element in their nature.... [And whereas] Blicher's young nobleman would have chosen death rather than hang his escutcheon round the neck of a pig, ... I am pretty sure that nowadays no nobleman in the world—anyway in one of the civilized countries,—would not be prepared to do so with a perfectly good conscience if thereby he could save his friends' lives, or even his own; for his highest duty is on a different plane. However deeply outraged a young woman might feel against an assailant who tried to rape her,—in the same degree as against a person who had burned down her house, for instance,—I think she would feel an even greater fury toward the people involved who assumed that she should feel herself degraded and 'dishonoured' by it.

By contrast, 'the women of the old days ... felt themselves to be representatives of something great and sacred, by virtue of which they possessed importance outside themselves and could feel great pride and dignity, and towards which they had a weighty responsibility ... I think very few women in our time feel any of this' (Dinesen 1983, pp. 336–7).

Isak Dinesen also provides us with the only version of the 'monstrous ransom' plot I know of wherein the heroine emerges absolutely unscathed, and with the highest of honours. Indeed, the only title Dinesen's tale *could* have is 'The Heroine'. The scene is (yet again) the border. A little group of priests and nuns and peasants, and a student of religious philosophy named Frederick Lamond, are attempting to get across to safety when a gloriously brave and beautiful woman joins them. The enemy commandant offers her the usual bargain. He will let the group across if she will come to him for the passports 'dressed like the goddess Venus'. 'Why do you ask me?' she asks him. 'Ask those who are with me.... Here is a French priest, ... the consoler of many poor souls; here are two French sisters, who have nursed the sick and dying. The two others have children in France, who will fare ill without them. Their salvation is, to each one of them, more important than mine'. The group decides that she must not go to the commandant, and she does not. The following morning, soldiers deliver papers permitting the group to cross the border, along with a bouquet of red roses addressed, with the commandant's compliments, 'To a heroine'.

Some time later, the student, Frederick, is taken to a show called *Diana's Triumph*, to see the most beautiful spectacle in Paris. To his astonishment, at the climax of the tableaux, the magnificent heroine of the journey appeared as 'the Goddess Diana herself, with nothing on at all'. The student goes backstage to reminisce about their journey, and asks her whether she had really believed she might be shot. 'Yes', said she. But the other members of the group faced 'a greater risk than that'. She had grown up among devout peasants and priests and nuns, and if they 'had bought their salvation at such a price', the priests and the old sister 'would never have got over it.' 'You', she says to the student, 'were not like the others'. If it had been only the two of them, he might have urged her to save their lives, 'in the way he told me, quite simply, and have thought nothing of it afterwards'. The commandant, 'she added thoughtfully', was 'an honest, an honest young man'. 'He could really want a thing. Many men have not got that in them.' 'Then your triumph', said the student 'was really all on our behalf? Because we had behaved so well?' 'You did behave well, did you not?' said she, smiling at him. 'So you were a greater heroine, even', said Frederick in the same way, 'than I knew at the time'.

And so the stakes involved in the 'monstrous ransom' plot have changed, and no doubt will change again. And the question 'Is there a point beyond which one must not go, not even to save one's own life, or to save another person?' has been answered in altogether different ways in different works of art. But it is just as well that few of us have to confront that question except in works of art. Discussing the ways differing prisoners confronted it, in a book based on his own experiences in Nazi concentration camps, Bruno Bettelheim answered it thus:

> To survive as a man, not a walking corpse, as a debased and degraded but still human being, one had first and foremost to remain informed and aware of what made up one's personal point of no return, the point beyond which one would never, under any circumstances, give in to the oppressor.... It meant being aware that if one survived at the price of overreaching this point one would be holding on to a life that had lost all its meaning. It would mean surviving—not with a lowered self-respect, but without any.
>
> (Bettelheim 1970, pp. 145–6)

This terrible recognition about life itself might help account for the merciful intervention of the Duke in *Measure for Measure*. Before that, Shakespeare himself takes Claudio and Isabella to 'the personal point of no return'. For their confrontation immediately before the Duke takes charge (see III.i. 55–152) suggests that had Isabella yielded to

Angelo, as Claudio urged her to do, they would never have
got over it: 'It would mean surviving—not with a lowered
self-respect, but without any.' Which may be the fate that
Angelo finds worse than death in the end.

The power of the 'monstrous ransom' plot has to do with
the forces that lie behind and beyond the physical or sexual
stakes. In a significant inversion of psychoanalytical
theories that reduce everything to, or explain everything
else in terms of, sexual motives or drives, in (say) *Boule de
Suif* as in *Measure for Measure*, sex serves as a metaphor for
different forces: for class oppression, for national pride; for
human dignity and freedom of choice; for the desire to raze
the sanctuary, for a desire for autonomy; for what's most
sacred, most profane; for the individual's point of no
return. When the stakes are lowered to the structural level,
as they were when J.R. told Sue Ellen to come to his bed, or
he'd have her lover jailed, in *Dallas*, the question, 'Should
she or shouldn't she?' is of structural importance only to the
next week's episode. She does, and that's that. Like the
young lover himself, the whole episode is soon forgotten,
and we think no more about it as the focus of the soap-opera
shifts in succeeding weeks. So far as I am concerned, the
opposite holds true in *Measure for Measure*: Shakespeare
raised the stakes, the *ante*, so high in portraying Angelo's
will to raze the sanctuary, and Isabella's desire to keep the
sacred unprofaned, that the lowering of the stakes in the
case of the bed-trick, like the shot-gun weddings in the end,
seems a kind of denial of individual dignity and freedom of
choice. But, again, it could be that the raising of extra-dramatic questions, and the play's strange tendency to arouse
(seemingly) unintended responses, may be what make us
feel certain, whatever else the play makes us feel uncertain
about, that *Measure for Measure* was written by a genius.

Select Bibliography

Altieri, Joanne. 'Style and Social Disorder in *Measure for Measure*', *Shakespeare Quarterly* 25 (1974), pp.6–16.

Barton, Anne. 'Measure for Measure', *The Riverside Shakespeare*, ed. G.B. Evans *et al.*, Boston 1974, pp.545–9. See also Righter, below.

Battenhouse, Roy W. '*Measure for Measure* and Christian Doctrine of the Atonement', *PMLA* 61 (1946), pp.1029–59.

Bawcutt, N.W., '"He Who the Sword of Heaven will Bear": The Duke versus Angelo in *Measure for Measure*', *Shakespeare Survey* 37 (1984), pp.88–97.

Bayley, John. *The Characters of Love*, London 1960. *The Uses of Division*, London 1976.

Beckerman, Bernard. 'A Shakespearean Experiment: The Dramaturgy of *Measure for Measure*', in *The Elizabethan Theatre II*, ed. David Galloway, Toronto 1970, pp.108–33.

Bennett, Josephine Waters. *Measure for Measure as Royal Entertainment*, New York 1966.

Berry, Ralph. 'Hierarchic Forms: Language and Structure in *Measure for Measure*', in *Shakespearean Structures*, London 1981, pp.47–63.

Bettelheim, Bruno. *The Informed Heart*, London 1970.

Borges, Jorge Luis. 'Tlön, Uqbar, Orbis Tertius', in

Labyrinths, ed. Donald A. Yates and James E. Irby, Harmondsworth 1970.

Bradbrook, Muriel C. 'Authority, Truth, and Justice in *Measure for Measure', Review of English Studies* 17 (1941), pp.385–99

'The Balance and the Sword in *Measure for Measure',* in *Artist and Society in Shakespeare's England,* vol.1, Brighton 1982, pp.144–54.

Bradley, A.C. *Shakespearean Tragedy,* London 1904.

Brecht, Bertolt, 'On *Macbeth, Hamlet, Lear', The Times Literary Supplement,* 23 April 1964.

Bronowski, J. *The Ascent of Man,* London 1973.

Burke, Kenneth. *A Grammar of Motives and a Rhetoric of Motives,* New York 1962.

Perspectives by Incongruity, ed. Stanley Edgar Hyman, Bloomington, Indiana, 1964.

Burton, Robert. *The Anatomy of Melancholy,* ed. Holbrook Jackson, London 1932.

Calderwood, James. *Shakespearean Metadrama,* Minneapolis, Minnesota, 1971.

Carter, Thomas. *Shakespeare and Holy Scripture, with the Version He Used,* London 1905.

Chekhov, Anton. *The Letters of Anton Chekhov,* ed. Avrahm Yarmolinsky, London 1974.

Chambers, E.K. *Shakespeare: A Survey,* London 1925.

Chambers, R.W. 'Measure for Measure', in *Man's Unconquerable Mind,* London 1939.

Coleridge, Samuel, *Lectures:* see Nicol Smith, 1916, pp.231–2.

Daiches, David. 'Guilt and Justice in Shakespeare', *Literary Essays,* Edinburgh, and London 1965.

Davenant, Sir William. *The Law Against Lovers,* in *Works,* 1673; reprinted in facsimile, London 1970.

Davies, Robertson. *World of Wonders,* in *The Deptford Trilogy,* Harmondsworth 1983.

Dinesen, Isak (Karen Blixen). 'Sorrow-acre' and 'The Heroine', in *Winter's Tales,* New York 1961.

Letters from Africa 1914–31, trans. Anne Born, London 1983. See also Thurman, below.

Dollimore, Jonathan. 'Transgression and Surveillance in *Measure for Measure*', in *Political Shakespeare: New Essays in Cultural Materialism*, ed. J. Dollimore and A. Sinfield, Manchester 1985.

Donaldson, Ian. *The World Upside-Down: Comedy from Jonson to Fielding*, Oxford 1970.

Dowden, Edward. *Shakespere: A Critical Study of His Mind and Art*, London 1875.

Eagleton, Terence. *Shakespeare and Society: Critical Studies in Shakespearian Drama*, London 1967.

William Shakespeare, Oxford 1986.

Eccles, Mark. *New Variorum Edition of Measure for Measure*, New York 1980.

Edwards, Philip. *Shakespeare and the Confines of Art*, London 1968.

Ellis-Fermor, U.M. *The Jacobean Drama: An Interpretation*, 1936.

Empson, William. *The Structure of Complex Words*, London 1951.

Milton's God, London 1961.

Evans, Bertrand. *Shakespeare's Comedies*, Oxford 1960.

Foakes, R.A. *Shakespeare. The Dark Comedies to the Last Plays: From Satire to Celebration*, London 1971.

French, A.L. *Shakespeare and the Critics*, Cambridge 1972.

French, Marilyn. *Shakespeare's Division of Experience*, London 1982.

Frye, Northrop. *The Myth of Deliverance: Reflections on Shakespeare's Problem Comedies*, Brighton 1983.

Frye, Roland M. *Shakespeare and Christian Doctrine*, Princeton, NJ 1963.

Garber, Marjorie. '"Wild Laughter in the Throat of Death"; Darker Purposes in Shakespearean Comedy', in *Shakespearean Comedy*, ed. Maurice Charney, *New York Literary Forum*, 1980, pp. 121–6.

Geckle, George L. 'Coleridge on *Measure for Measure*',

Shakespeare Quarterly 18 (1967), pp. 71–3.

(ed.) *Twentieth Century Interpretations of Measure for Measure*, Englewood Cliffs, 1970.

Gervinus, G.*Shakespeare Commentaries*, trans. F.E. Bunnètt, 1875; reprinted New York 1971.

Gildon, Charles. *Measure for Measure, or Beauty the Best Advocate*, 1700; reprinted in facsimile, London 1969.

Gill, Brendan, *Tallulah*, London 1972.

Gless, Darryl J. *Measure for Measure: The Law and the Convent*, Princeton, NJ, 1979.

Goldman, Michael. *Shakespeare and the Energies of the Drama*, London 1972.

Hamilton, Donna B. 'The Duke in *Measure for Measure*', *Shakespeare Studies* 6 (1970), pp. 175–83.

Harding, Davis P. 'Elizabethan Betrothals and *Measure for Measure*', *Journal of English and Germanic Philology* 49 (1950), pp. 139–58.

Hawkes, Terence. *Shakespeare and the Reason: A Study of the Tragedies and the Problem Plays*, London 1964.

Hazlitt, William. *Characters of Shakespear's Plays*, 2nd edn, 1818.

Hill, Christopher. *Irreligion in the 'Puritan' Revolution*, London 1974.

Hobbes, Thomas. *Leviathan*, ed. C.B. Macpherson, Harmondsworth 1968.

Honigmann, E.A.J. *Shakespeare: The 'Lost Years'*, Manchester 1985.

Hunter, G.K. 'Six Notes on *Measure for Measure*', *Shakespeare Quarterly* 15 (1964), pp. 167–72.

(ed.) *All's Well That Ends Well*, New Arden Shakespeare, London 1959.

Hunter, R.G. *Shakespeare and the Comedy of Forgiveness*, New York 1965.

Jardine, Lisa. *Still Harping on Daughters: Women and Drama in the Age of Shakespeare*, Brighton 1983.

Jonson, Ben. *The Works of Ben Jonson*, ed. C.H. Herford and Percy and Evelyn Simpson, Oxford 1925–52.

Kauffmann, R.J. 'Bond Slaves and Counterfeits': Shakespeare's *Measure for Measure*, *Shakespeare Studies* 3 (1967), pp.85–97.

Kirsch, Arthur C. 'The Integrity of *Measure for Measure*', *Shakespeare Survey* 28 (1975), pp.89–105.

Knight, G. Wilson. '*Measure for Measure* and the Gospels', in *The Wheel of Fire*, London 1949.

Knights, L.C. 'The Ambiguity of *Measure for Measure*', *Scrutiny* 10 (1942), pp.222–33.

Kott, Jan. 'Head for Maidenhead, Maidenhead for Head: The Structure of Exchange in *Measure for Measure*', *Theatre Quarterly* 8 (1978), pp.18–24.

Lascelles, Mary. *Shakespeare's 'Measure for Measure'*, London 1953.

Lavin, J.A. '*Measure for Measure*', *Stratford Papers* 1968–9, ed. B.A.W. Jackson, Hamilton, Ontario, Canada, and Shannon, Ireland 1972, pp.97–113.

Lawrence, W.W. *Shakespeare's Problem Comedies*, New York 1931.

Leavis, F.R. '*Measure for Measure*', in *The Common Pursuit*, London 1952.

Leonard, Nancy S. 'Substitutions in Shakespeare's Problem Comedies', *English Literary Renaissance* 9 (1979), pp.281–301.

Lever, J.W. (ed.) *Measure for Measure*, New Arden Shakespeare, London 1965.

Levin, Richard, *New Readings vs. Old Plays: Recent Trends in the Reinterpretation of English Renaissance Drama*, Chicago 1979.

Machiavelli, Niccolò. *The Prince*, trans. Robert M. Adams, New York 1977.

Mahood, M.M. *Shakespeare's Wordplay*, London 1957.

'"Unblotted Lines": Shakespeare at Work', *Publications of the British Academy*, 58 (1972), pp.163–76.

Maupassant, Guy de. *Boule de Suif and Other Stories*, trans. H.N.P. Sloman, Harmondsworth 1946.

Maxwell, J. C. '*Measure for Measure*: The Play and the

Themes', British Academy Shakespeare Lecture, Oxford 1974.

McLuskie, Kathleen. 'The Patriarchal Bard: Feminist Criticism and Shakespeare: *King Lear* and *Measure for Measure*', in *Political Shakespeare: New Essays in Cultural Materialism* ed. J. Dollimore and A. Sinfield, London 1985.

Medawar, Sir Peter. *The Art of the Soluble*, London 1967.

Melville, Herman. *Billy Budd*, ed. Frederic Freeman and Elizabeth Treeman, Cambridge, Mass. 1956.

Miles, Rosalind. *The Problem of 'Measure for Measure': A Historical Investigation*, London 1976.

Milton, John. *The Doctrine and Discipline of Divorce, Areopagitica*, and *Tetrachordon*, in *The Complete Prose Works of John Milton*, vol.2., 1643–8, ed. Ernest Sirluck, New Haven, Conn. 1959 (I have modernised the prose quotations from Milton in my text).

Mincoff, Marco. '*Measure for Measure*: A Question of Approach', *Shakespeare Studies* 2 (1966), pp.141–52.

Morgann, Maurice. *Shakespeare Criticism*, ed. Daniel A. Fineman, Oxford 1972.

Muir, Kenneth. *Shakespeare's Sources*, vol.1, *Comedies and Tragedies*, London 1957.

The Sources of Shakespeare's Plays, London 1977.

Shakespeare's Comic Sequence, Liverpool 1979.

and Wells, Stanley (eds) *Aspects of Shakespeare's 'Problem Plays'*, Cambridge 1982.

Nagarajan, S. '*Measure for Measure* and Elizabethan Betrothals', *Shakespeare Quarterly* 14 (1963), pp.115–19.

(ed.) *Measure for Measure*, Signet Classic Shakespeare, New York 1964.

Neely, Carol Thomas. *Broken Nuptials in Shakespeare's Plays*, New Haven, Conn., and London 1985.

Nicholls, Graham. *Measure for Measure: Text and Performance*, London 1986.

Nicol Smith, D. *Shakespeare Criticism, A Selection*

1623–1840, London 1916.

Novy, Marianne. *Love's Argument: Gender Relations in Shakespeare*, Chapel Hill and London 1984.

Nuttall, A.D. '*Measure for Measure*: Quid pro Quo?', *Shakespeare Studies* 4 (1968), pp.231–51.

'*Measure for Measure*: The Bed-trick', *Shakespeare Survey* 28 (1975), pp.51–6.

Ornstein, Robert. *The Moral Vision of Jacobean Tragedy*, Madison, Wisconsin, 1960.

(ed.) *Discussions of Shakespeare's Problem Comedies*, Boston 1961.

Pasternak Slater, Ann. *Shakespeare the Director*, Brighton 1982.

Pope, Elizabeth M. 'The Renaissance Background of *Measure for Measure*', *Shakespeare Survey* 2 (1949), pp.66–82 (reprinted in Geckle, and in Muir and Wells).

Price, Hereward T. 'Construction in Shakespeare', *University of Michigan Contributions in Modern Philology*, no.17, Ann Arbor, Michigan, 1951.

Rees, Joan. *Shakespeare and the Story: Aspects of Creation*, London 1978.

Riefer, Marcia. '"Instruments of Some More Mightier Member": The Constriction of Female Power in *Measure for Measure*', *Shakespeare Quarterly* 35 (1984), pp.157–69.

Righter, Anne. *Shakespeare and the Idea of the Play*, London 1962. See also Barton, above.

Rose, Jacqueline. 'Sexuality in the Reading of Shakespeare: *Hamlet* and *Measure for Measure*', in *Alternative Shakespeares*, ed. John Drakakis, London 1985.

Rossiter, A.P. *Angel with Horns and Other Shakespeare Lectures*, ed. Graham Storey, London 1961.

Sacks, Elizabeth. *Shakespeare's Images of Pregnancy*, London 1980.

Schanzer, Ernst. 'The Marriage-Contracts in *Measure for Measure*', *Shakespeare Survey* 13 (1960), pp.81–9.

The Problem Plays of Shakespeare, London 1963.

Schleiner, Louise. 'Ethical Improvisation in *Measure for Measure*', PMLA 97 (1982), pp. 227–36.

Scott, Sir Walter. *The Heart of Midlothian*, ed. Claire Lamont, Oxford 1982.

Scouten, Arthur H. 'An Historical Approach to *Measure for Measure*', *Philological Quarterly* 54 (1975), pp. 68–84.

Sisson, C. J. 'The Mythical Sorrows of Shakespeare', *Proceedings of the British Academy* 20 (1934), pp. 45–70.

Skura, Meredith Anne. *The Literary Use of the Psychoanalytic Process*, New Haven, Conn., and London 1981.

Stevenson, D. L. *The Achievement of Shakespeare's 'Measure for Measure'*, Ithaca, NY 1966.

Summers, Joseph H. *Dreams of Love and Power: On Shakespeare's Plays*, Oxford 1984.

Thurman, Judith. *Isak Dinesen: The Life of Karen Blixen*, London 1982.

Tillyard, E. M. W. *Shakespeare's Problem Plays*, London 1950.

Watts, Cedric. *Measure for Measure*, Penguin Masterstudies, Harmondsworth 1986.

Weil, Herbert S., Jr. 'Form and Contexts in Measure for Measure', *Critical Quarterly* 12 (1970), pp. 55–72.

'The Options of the Audience: Theory and Practice in Peter Brook's *Measure for Measure*', *Shakespeare Survey* 25 (1972), pp. 27–35.

Wentersdorf, Karl P. 'The Marriage Contracts in *Measure for Measure*: A Reconsideration', *Shakespeare Survey* 32 (1979), pp. 129–44.

Index